TRANSFORMATIVE LEARNING
THROUGH ENGAGEMENT

TRANSFORMATIVE LEARNING THROUGH ENGAGEMENT

Student Affairs Practice as Experiential Pedagogy

Jane Fried and Associates

Foreword by James E. Zull

STERLING, VIRGINIA

COPYRIGHT © 2012 BY
STYLUS PUBLISHING, LLC.

Published by Stylus Publishing, LLC
22883 Quicksilver Drive
Sterling, Virginia 20166-2102

Library of Congress Cataloging-in-Publication Data
Fried, Jane.
 Transformative learning through engagement : student affairs practice as experiential pedagogy / Jane Fried and Associates.—First Edition.
     pages   cm
 Includes bibliographical references and index.
 ISBN 978-1-57922-758-6 (cloth : alk. paper)
 ISBN 978-1-57922-759-3 (pbk. : alk. paper)
 ISBN 978-1-57922-760-9 (library networkable e-edition)
 ISBN 978-1-57922-761-6 (consumer e-edition)
 1. Student affairs services—United States.   2. Learning, Psychology of.   3. College teaching—United States.
I. Title.
LB2342.9.F76   2012
378.1′94—dc23   2011043692

13-digit ISBN: 978-1-57922-758-6 (cloth)
13-digit ISBN: 978-1-57922-759-3 (paper)
13-digit ISBN: 978-1-57922-760-9 (library networkable e-edition)
13-digit ISBN: 978-1-57922-761-6 (consumer e-edition)

Printed in the United States of America

All first editions printed on acid free paper
that meets the American National Standards Institute
Z39-48 Standard.

Bulk Purchases

Quantity discounts are available for use in workshops
and for staff development.
Call 1-800-232-0223

First Edition, 2012

10   9   8   7   6   5   4   3   2

This book is offered to all students everywhere.
May each student find mentors
who help them discover their gifts
and learn how to use them
for the welfare of humanity.

I am thankful to all my mentors and
hold them in love and appreciation.

Burns Crookston

Donna Fairfield

Doris Perry

Mabel and Ted Smith

Muriel King Taylor

All others seen and unseen

CONTENTS

ACKNOWLEDGMENTS

M y thanks go to the American College Personnel Association and Harold Cheatham, past chair of the Editorial Board, for their support of *Shifting Paradigms in Student Affairs*, forerunner to this book; to the National Association of Student Personnel Administrators and executive director Gwen Dungy, who supported the writing of *Learning Reconsidered 1* and *2*, which allowed me to think more deeply about transformative learning; and to the Barre Center for Buddhist Studies, where I learned to appreciate the many connections between brain function and meditation and also realized that the mysteries are never fully understood.

FOREWORD

Fried presents the following challenge:

> A major difficulty in higher education arises from the growing diversity of learners and their experiences, particularly outside the classroom. In contrast, the subject experts (teachers) tend to view their material itself as homogeneous (chemistry is chemistry), and unrelated (or weakly related) to the learner's views and experiences. The result of this "missing of the minds" often leads students to feel that their education is irrelevant, or disconnected from "the real world."

However, as Fried explains, universities do have a cadre of experts who understand this diversity and the impact it has on learning. Currently, those experts are found primarily in what have been labeled "offices of student affairs." Fried suggests integrating their expertise with that of the teachers, and argues that this would "transform" higher education.

As I read *Transformative Learning Through Engagement*, I began to recognize my own ignorance. I was forced to acknowledge that I wasn't sure myself what these student affairs offices do—what are they experts in? So I checked out the student affairs website at my own university. As I encountered terms like *student development, service learning, co-op, career counseling*, and *first year experience*, it dawned on me. This was about experiential learning; something I should have realized, having written two books along those lines!

One of my points of confusion was that I linked counseling and tutoring with student affairs. In my mind, I saw student affairs as more about helping troubled students than about proactive challenge initiatives. If I had a problem student, I might send them to student affairs. But if I wanted a new way to teach biochemistry, I would turn to my science colleagues in the faculty. But now I wonder if my misunderstandings might not be mine alone. Maybe they are typical of those colleagues. They, perhaps, might see themselves as separate from student affairs. We were the scholars and creators in the disciplines. Student affairs were not intellectual affairs.

So it was that Fried began to challenge this impression. In fact, her pro-posals began to sound a great deal like an idea I had thought about for some time: maybe all of our university constituencies, faculty and students, would benefit from studying the process that we call learning, with a course on learning for beginning students, as well as for beginning faculty? We had something along these lines in our special programs for new faculty mem-bers, offered through our center for teaching and learning. Maybe we should expand that.

*   *   *

The foundation for a change like that would almost certainly be a particular theory of learning called *constructivism*. The core idea in this theory is that learners in any context construct their own understandings from their per-sonal and unique experiences. Thus, teachers may be greatly helped by using pedagogy that includes, and builds on, that prior knowledge. A new peda-gogical model emerges. In this model, students, professors, and student affairs professionals work together, seeking ways for the student to build on her prior knowledge; not only her subject knowledge, but also her knowl-edge of herself, obtained by her unique and personal experiences; the major source of that troublesome diversity.

This understanding of learning itself is something the student affairs professional can bring to the table—something that the academic expert, the biochemist, the historian, the mathematician, does not. Fried suggests that this expertise can be utilized more effectively if everyone works together with this common goal. We might establish new administrative structures, new protocols, or new behaviors that are designed to bring the subject-expertise together with the learning-expertise. Such a response could catalyze a syner-gistic dynamic that engages the prior knowledge of everyone, not just the student's.

This proposal raises, at least, two primary questions, one theoretical, and one operational. First, is it true that learning and knowledge are constructed, rather than delivered? Is construction the best goal for the teacher? Are the mechanisms of learning documented well enough to be used with confi-dence? Second, what structures or mechanisms would facilitate and support such a proactive initiative? Or, would the administrative structure of the uni-versity prevent such dynamic and innovative change? Will we be able to overcome the divisions that I described previously? Or would the barriers, both physical and experiential, keep them separated physically, intellectually, and psychologically? In what follows I address both of these questions.

First, let's focus on the question about learning. In past work, I have argued that we do understand important aspects of the learning process. I don't claim that we know every detail, every possible complication, or all the complexities and differences in individual cases, but some fundamentals are clear. These fundamentals are neurological in nature. They are about the brain. They begin with the notion that knowledge is physical. It consists of physical structures known as neuronal networks. This is a generalization about all people, not just the student. The claim is that more than simply representing knowledge, these networks are, themselves, knowledge. And, accepting that claim, it follows that learning is a physical change in these networks—change in knowledge! This change can consist of adding new neurons to a network; eliminating neurons in a network; inhibiting or activating existing networks; or, similarly, creating or eliminating whole networks. These fundamental claims describe the physical basis for the constructivism theory of learning.

We can see, then, a pedagogical method embedded in these claims. To help people learn, we must first know about their current knowledge and beliefs. Achieving that, we must know what generates change in such brain networks. And for stable learning we must know what leads to long-term change—to memory. The research about these questions points strongly to *repetition* and *emotion*. Effective pedagogy must be designed to engage existing networks, and to use them repeatedly, with focus. It must utilize repetition. And, perhaps of greatest importance, our pedagogy must engage the emotions. The neuroscience evidence strongly suggests the importance of this additional factor. Hundreds of experiments have demonstrated that change in neuron connections is most effective when powerful, but ancient emotion systems are part of the response.

The key terms in this type of pedagogy are *prior, knowledge, engaging*, and *emotion*. The "prior" aspect comes from creating stable changes in networks; the "knowledge" aspect resides in the physical network itself; the revision and repetition of prior knowledge provides for continually "engaging" the existing networks; and the personal nature of the knowledge activates the "emotions" through well-known chemical systems in the brain such as those dependent on dopamine or serotonin.

The second challenge, the operational aspects of bringing folks together, suggests a number of possibilities. I will point out two. First, we might reexamine the existing organizational structure inherent in educational institutions, particularly those in the United States. As Fried says, offices of student affairs frequently are established and administered separately from academic departments and colleges. We separate the learning experts from the teaching experts, physically as well as cognitively and experientially. But as I have tried to point out, highly professional student affairs experts also are more likely to have deep insight into the constructivist nature of learning than are academics. In fact, subject experts who become teachers (academics) do not necessarily credit constructivism, and indeed may never have heard of it. Thus, we might consider an administrative merger of faculty and student affairs. Although extreme, such a merger would send a powerful message about the mission of universities—we are learning institutions.

A less dramatic and problematic approach would be to establish teams of educators consisting of subject experts and learning experts. Such teams might be created to align with the current academic structures, such as departments, or with schools or divisions of sciences and humanities. Either way, these teams would be established based on the notion that the combination of student affairs professionals and subject experts appears to offer the best chance to support the student.

Fried's suggestion that academics and administrators should work closely together, maybe even merge, has merit. It is consistent with our knowledge of learning and it confronts a real and growing challenge. True, it is daunting (and thus brave) but we should take it seriously. We may encounter those old enemies inertia, habit, and attitude, but let's hope that the need for serious change, so strongly supported by Fried, brings it to the attention of energized and creative professionals in higher education.

James E. Zull
Director of The University Center for Innovation in Teaching and
Education (UCITE) at Case Western Reserve University

PART ONE

SHIFTING PARADIGMS
IN EDUCATION

I

INSIGHT

Perspectives on Learning

The Universe is a self-organizing system engaged in the discovery of its possibilities through a continuing process of transcendence toward ever higher levels of order and self-definition.

(Korten, 1999, p. 12)

Q uestion: What would universities look like if they consisted of groups of people with training in specific areas of inquiry who came together to explore areas of ongoing human concern? What if these groups included more-advanced and less-advanced scholars? What if problems were posed, and searching for solutions informed pedagogy? What if all people involved formulated the problems and then collaborated on developing answers? How would that translate into an organizational structure? Would inexperienced people who have not learned to structure their work be allowed to participate? Would people have to be located in the same physical place? Could a virtual seminar replace one that occurred in a physical location? Would anything be lost? What might we discover if we started by asking questions about the ways we organize learning rather than looking for answers about the best way to organize teaching?

Image from *War and Peace* (Tolstoy, 1869)
This globe was alive—a vibrating ball without fixed dimensions. Its whole surface consisted of drops closely pressed together, and all these drops moved and changed places, sometimes several of them merging into one, sometimes one dividing into many. Each drop tried to spread out and

3

occupy as much space as possible, but others striving to do the same compressed it, sometimes destroyed it, and sometimes merged with it. "That is life," said the old teacher. "How simple and clear it is," thought Pierre. "How is it I did not know it before?" God is in the midst, and each drop tries to expand so as to reflect Him to the greatest extent. And it grows, merges, disappears from the surface, sinks to the depths, and again emerges. (Tolstoy, 1869/2011, p. 2595)

Pierre attributed this process to God. Today modern physicists might substitute other terms such as *field, energy pattern, coherent system*, or *holon* (Laszlo, 2006) to signify an organically coherent system, which is "integrated and dynamic, its myriad activities self-motivated, self-organizing and spontaneous, engaging all levels simultaneously from the microscopic and molecular all the way to the macroscopic" (p. 93). The notion of coherence can be applied to all kinds of systems, biological, social, and organizational, and is often described as ecology.

The current image of a university is neither coherent nor organic. It seems to combine medieval processes with industrial age content. Our image of learning is medieval—auditory, reified knowledge being transmitted via the spoken and written word to listeners who transcribe or summarize. Lecturing precludes interaction among learners over questions and reifies knowledge in static form for emission and transmission. The organizational structure is a combination of Julius Caesar's legionary bureaucracy and Ford's automobile assembly line, accumulating credits via linear progress in order to produce an "educated" person at the end. The notion of getting an education makes this image reified. Our industrial-era institutions are actually modeled on a proposal made by Immanuel Kant (1798/1979) in *The Conflict of the Faculties*. Kant identified two key purposes for modern universities: to produce well-educated bureaucrats to manage the emerging nation-states, and to create knowledge for emerging industry that was based on the application of scientific information to industrial problems. Pedagogy was emphatically reserved for the gymnasia, or high schools. Teaching was not a concern of universities. The historical purpose of liberal education—liberating minds to explore multiple perspectives on the human condition and human projects—was ignored. Students were prepared for management roles in state bureaucracies, not for leadership in communities. In this process, helping students understand and critique the Grand Narrative of their own civilization was minimized or lost, and students were left on their own to place themselves in a meaningful cultural context (Readings, 1996).

The postcorporate, postindustrial, postmodern world is organized very differently from the industrial world. The world of factories, bureaucracies, and assembly lines is rigid, linear, slow, and fragmented. The postmodern environment is fluid, flexible, networked, and responds to change rapidly. Our current society is facing an entirely new set of problems, and students in this world have a very different set of skills and needs from those of Kant's era. Our educational institutions also have access to teaching/learning technologies that were never dreamed of in the early industrial era. We are now in a position to assume that oral transmission of information is rarely necessary, and that new knowledge generated to address all kinds of issues can be produced in a variety of locations and communicated among researchers in real time. This society needs to generate knowledge that addresses current problems, to apply that knowledge to problems, and to use the results of the solutions to create subsequent solutions in an endless loop. We have little need to transmit knowledge that may be out of date before students have an opportunity to use it. The form, the process, and the fundamental assumptions of most of our modern universities are profoundly out of date. They are also extremely expensive and may become unsustainable in the near future (Taylor, 2010). Widely used teaching/learning processes (i.e., lecturing/listening, test taking, and reading paper texts) almost guarantee the obsolescence of what is learned before the learning is assessed. Some of the most demanding and complex problems of our times cannot be studied in the isolation of university learning environments because addressing these problems demands learning from their complexity in real time and using well-informed intelligence to generate possible approaches and solutions. From economics to ecosystems, from cross-cultural communication to the management of global business, we must develop approaches to learning that integrate theoretical knowledge, empirical data, and personal experience.

The current learning model separates theory, data, and personal experience, and emphasizes theory and data while generally ignoring personal experience. More and more exceptions to this model are being developed in North America (O'Sullivan, 1999), but the historical model of teaching and learning conforms to these outlines. The notion that teaching involves speaking to students about knowledge that has already been developed remains the dominant methodology in universities. The set of questions raised by Korten's (1999) analysis of the postcorporate world can be applied to universities with illuminating results. Korten's vision evokes learning communities, not colleges or universities as we have created them for the past millennium. These kinds of learning communities can be compared to Tolstoy's. They are holons, systems that are complete within themselves and also part of larger systems. Holons interact with other holons, merge to address salient problems , and share intellectual and physical resources. They are organized via networks, electronic, organic, interpersonal, or mechanical. They fragment when creating applied solutions to particular problems in particular places. Their members' lives include academic work but also other dimensions of life and do not include adolescent ghettos generally referred to as residence halls. In a college designed as a learning community, the almost universal distinction between academic affairs (learning) and student affairs (living) would diminish or disappear; the community would focus on learning as a coherent process.

Transformative Learning as the Educational Role of Student Affairs

Since the publication of *Shifting Paradigms in Student Affairs* (Fried & Associates, 1995), a work that discussed learning as an integrated process and the role of student affairs as one experiential component of that process, much has been discovered about human learning (Zull, 2002). Student affairs professionals have attempted to shift their focus to include student learning in their mission and purpose (Keeling, 2004) but seem to have emphasized the assessment of learning outcomes without developing a similar emphasis on the creation and design of learning experiences or inputs. Student affairs professionals have a long history of attempting to understand and explain the educational role of student affairs yet have not been able to shift the focus from student services, which colleges assign to student affairs staff, to student learning, which colleges tend to assign solely to academic faculty. The earliest articulation of this shift appeared in 1938 (Lloyd-Jones & Smith), although the first description of the idea appeared in *The Student Personnel Point of View* (*SPPV*; American Council on Education, 1937). Lloyd-Jones was one of the primary authors of that document and expanded her ideas in her 1938 book. *A Student Personnel Program for Higher Education* (Lloyd-Jones & Smith) appeared in 1938. Since the publication of the *SPPV*, the educational mission of the student affairs profession has embraced training students for their role as effective citizens in an increasingly complex democracy. That role has not changed, although the demands have become more complicated. The notion of national citizenship has been expanded to include planetary citizenship and ecological responsibility or sustainability as well. A review of the Lloyd-Jones and Smith writings raises a powerful question. If these writings are universally revered by student affairs professionals, why has so little been done to shift the governing paradigm of student affairs work since the 1930s when these ideas began to appear in our literature? Why does the student affairs profession frame its work primarily in terms of services and only secondarily in terms of education for citizenship? What is the barrier that keeps student affairs as a profession from presenting itself to the academy as the experiential component of higher education, the component that contributes profoundly to the mission of almost every college in the United States, to educate citizens for effective participation in democracy (Fried, 2011)? *Transformative Learning Through Engagement* is an attempt to address that question.

Since the publication of *Shifting Paradigms in Student Affairs* (Fried & Associates, 1995), I have benefitted from the enormous insights into learning that have been developed over the past decades. Zull (2002) has discussed the correspondence between the neurology of learning and Kolb's (1984) description of the action/reflection learning cycle. Jensen (2000) has described the learning process and the process of designing brain-based learning. Mezirow and Associates (2000) and O'Sullivan (1999) have described transformative learning as the process by which individuals become aware of their phenomenological assumptions and then learn to explore their own processes of knowledge construction. In *The Mindful Brain* Siegel (2007) described in great detail "top-down . . . engrained brain states" (p. 135) that shape our perception of experience and information. He uses the word "enslavement" (p. 137) to describe our own preconceived ideas and asserts that this mental incarceration often keeps us from learning or changing our minds. Siegel also described the role that fear plays in keeping people entrapped in their own unexamined ideas and has seen the physiology of stereotyping in action on functional magnetic resonance imaging (fMRI) scans of the brain.

Dismantling mental architecture is difficult whether we are asking White American students to explore their culturally inculcated racism or asking heterosexual people to explore their prejudices about gay people. How much more difficult a task is it when we ask students who have never thought of themselves as anything other than Americans to begin expanding their idea of *we* to include people in other countries they may never meet, whose beliefs seem strange to them, and who live under circumstances in families that bear little resemblance to what traditional Americans think of as normal. This learning process becomes even more complex if our typical American students see people from some other part of the world as potential enemies because fear inhibits learning and empathy.

The philosophical and biological foundations have been laid for us to create a coherent approach to learning in higher education. What Lloyd-Jones and Smith (1954) described in fairly imprecise terms decades ago can now be described in very detailed terminology. These approaches can be implemented wherever educators are willing to redesign their work so that it is grounded in organic learning processes. We may divide our institutions into academic affairs and student affairs, but students learn as whole human beings. What is needed in the 21st century is a new approach to learning in higher education that is grounded in the science of learning. This gives students the opportunities to critique the inherited knowledge of previous generations so they can perceive new problems accurately and generate new solutions to the issues of their own lives. Our students have access to more information than any other generation in the history of our species. However, for information to be transformed into knowledge and possibly to wisdom, students must develop "a meaningful degree of understanding" (Glisczinski, 2007, p. 317) that allows them to critique what they are learning and dismantle their top-down mental architecture.

The only way to open minds in the fashion that so many educators value is to integrate our approaches to learning. Preconceived ideas and their accompanying neural architecture must be challenged in as many contexts as necessary, involving as many areas of the brain as possible. Burns Crookston (1975) suggested an approach to integrating the entire learning environment to reflect the organic nature of learning. He described three sets of interrelated competencies: instruction, consultation, and milieu management. He defined instruction as including teaching and research, and assigned that competency to academic faculty. Consultation involved all the elements of group process, helping people and groups clarify goals and learn to work together to achieve mutually determined goals, which is generally the kind of work that most student affairs professionals do on a daily basis. Milieu management, a role he assigned to chief student affairs officers, involves understanding all aspects of the organization that contribute to student learning. This understanding leads to the coordination and integration of the total campus environment to support the development of a democratic community in which all participants have the skills to act as contributing members of that community. Crookston asserted that all people who are professionally involved in higher education should have all these competencies, although each group has a specific area of responsibility in which its level of skill is presumed to be higher. This is an early description of a collaborative approach to supporting student learning throughout the campus for the purposes of helping students see themselves as contributing members of a democratic society.

This volume uses an analysis of culture, power, prejudice, and justice to illustrate the processes of organic brain-based learning. Diversity education or social justice training is typically the responsibility of the student affairs staff on most campuses. Had effective methods been in use for helping people replace their closed systems of thinking about people in predefined categories such as race, gender, sexual orientation, and ability status, there would probably be less need for continuing education about diversity and justice. However, the need remains great, and there is no consistent understanding of the kind of learning that contributes to the dismantling of top-down, enslaving mental architecture (Siegel, 2007) that translates into prejudicial ideas and harassing or condescending behavior. The incidents of intergroup conflict and misunderstanding on campuses continue, and microaggressions have increased, even if outright hostility seems to have diminished (Sue et al., 2007). Keeling's (2004) *Learning Reconsidered* provided the latest element in this conversation for student affairs professionals. Learning and transformation in higher education is intended to provide the next stage in this dialogue.

Purposes of This Volume

The overarching purpose of this book is to introduce all people who are professionally involved in helping college students learn to develop a basic understanding of the learning process, particularly those elements that include behavioral changes and the ability to place information in a broader context of personal meaning and long-term consequences. The ideas in this book speak to people who realize how profoundly out of date the industrial model of higher education has become. These professionals, who may be either student affairs professionals or academic faculty, have become frustrated with the alienation of so many students from their own academic learning because they do not understand the reasons they are required to study certain subjects. This problem is often described as "getting the gen ed requirements out of the way so students can get into their major," which is presumably the subject students are interested in.

A second purpose of this book is to provide information for student affairs professionals so they can articulate their own roles in helping students learn. Student affairs as a profession has had difficulty describing its work with students as teaching because the dominant paradigm of teaching continues to suggest a classroom, an academic expert, and a model of learning that is basically verbal and cognitive. After reading this book, student affairs professionals will be able to understand and describe the processes of experiential transformative education to their academic colleagues and help design integrated learning experiences as partners with academic faculty. This knowledge and experience will support ongoing efforts to create authentic assessment of learning in all domains of higher education. People who want to use off-the-shelf training programs will probably not be motivated to understand the complexity of the learning process or to create experiential education activities for specific learning needs on particular campuses. This is not a cookbook. It is a brief explanation of the science of experiential learning, coupled with an analysis of cultural norms. All this information can be combined to produce transformative learning experiences in the domain of civic engagement, particularly processes involved with community leadership and service.

Finally, the information contained in this book can serve as a stimulus for conversation among faculty and staff members who are beginning to design integrated, transformative learning programs for their own campuses. These collaborative conversations must occur, whether programs are divided into separate but coordinated academic and experiential components, or whether they are integrated, team-taught courses that involve experiences that bring classroom-based concepts to life. Collaboration is vital to the development of the integrated transformative approach described in this book. "Collaboration forms a network of ideas and resources that not only supports student learning, but also creates a collegial infrastructure . . . [as well as] the development of mutual language and shared assumptions about the value, importance and support of student learning" (Steffes & Keeling,

2006, p. 69). Implementation of such collaborative processes has the potential to transform campus culture and our common understanding of learning, thus revitalizing our experiences in higher education.

Organization of the Book

Part One includes a summary of the key elements of learning from the perspective of cognitive neuroscience. It also includes an analysis of American culture and the enculturation process, which leads to an inquiry about methods dismantling these beliefs when they are destructive. Part Two moves from the author's analysis of American culture and learning processes to the reader's experience of both phenomena. Readers are requested to cocreate an understanding and learning experience so they can begin to use what they know.

The chapters in Part Three by contributing authors describe a number of emerging models and programs that integrate experience, study, and reflection to produce powerful, engaged, and transformative learning experiences for students.

2

LABELS AND VIEWPOINTS

Lenses That Shape Learning

S tudent Affairs and Services, as professional nomenclature, reflects a long-standing split in the responsibilities of the field. The domain and responsibilities of student service areas are fairly clear. That segment of our work offers the services students need to access a wide range of institutional resources from admissions and financial aid to housing, food service, and registration. Student affairs, on the other hand, is much less clear in either its definition or its range of responsibilities (Fried, 2010). What is student affairs and how is it different from student development or student development education? Student affairs seems to cover everything that is associated with student needs, student behavior, and student activities. The term generally refers to all kinds of advising, training for peer advisers and student leaders, student conduct, and training in the career selection and job search process. I was once responsible for the Office of Off-Campus Student Affairs, an off-campus housing office. In 1972 this terminology led to many entertaining conversations with faculty and other staff members about how far a college should go in supervising and providing services for students.

Names matter. Names signify frames of reference, paradigms and assumptions, beliefs about what will happen or what something means. Latino/Latina people have powerful opinions about whether they want to be considered Latino/Latina, Hispanic, or hyphenated Americans with a signifier that indicates their family's country of origin. There are significant differences in meaning between the terms *African American*, *Negro*, and *nigger*. Jews know the difference between *Jewish* and *kike*, even if the latter term has fallen out of use. Names matter.

The pace of change in higher education and throughout society has been accelerating rapidly since the end of World War II. Since evolutionary change does not proceed at the same pace as social and technological change, humans have developed mechanisms like multitasking and information searches on the Internet to stay ahead of the curve. Despite the increasing tidal wave of knowledge, the paradigm that shapes higher education institutions has changed very little. Even in places where a great deal of technology has been introduced, the technology is generally used to reinforce the traditional mission and processes of higher education—the creation, transmission, retention, and use of information. Since the paradigm that governs most knowledge development and transmission has historically been positivist, the effects of perspective on knowledge have not been generally acknowledged or discussed. Concurrently, students are using new technologies to do their own research, and this frequently exposes them to different perspectives and interpretations of information. They are often interacting with friends, reading the news, and listening to music or surfing YouTube at the same time they are acquiring information in class via academic lectures. Blogging has removed the editorial function from much of what is published, and there is little a priori guarantee of credibility from many news sources in the blogosphere. Students in the wired world simply cannot avoid being aware of multiple perspectives. At the same time that I have been writing this chapter, I have also been searching for a clear definition of positivism and stopping briefly to find out what the stock market was doing. I remind the reader that I am nearing retirement, which is why I am concerned about the stock market, and I do not have a fraction of the skill in multitasking that our students in their 20s do.

The changes in volume, availability, and range of information that have occurred because of the technological revolution have undermined some of the positivist foundations of Western secular higher education. Positivism is an epistemological frame of reference in which "the goal of knowledge is simply to describe the phenomena that we experience" (Trochim, 2000). Two foundational assumptions are that perspective does not, or should not, influence knowledge, and that emotions, or what we might call caring about what is being learned, often interfere with accurate understanding. Both of these elements are grounded in positivist epistemology and are so embedded in the paradigm of traditional doctoral training and undergraduate instruction that they are often invisible and unremarked. If the goal of knowledge is to describe what exists, what methods do we have for helping our students learn how to differentiate between varying descriptions of what exists? How do we help them develop standards for credibility in a world where photo-shopping is synonymous with altering a photograph to create effects that never existed in the physical world?

It seems that one critical role of higher education in the shaping of our students' cognitive, affective, and behavioral development is to help them become aware of their own assumptions about what exists (Bok, 2006; Mezirow & Associates, 2000). This process is typically described as becoming aware of lenses or frames of reference, the evaluative criteria students use when assessing the credibility of information. Learning to become aware of and to reflect critically on the lenses through which we view the world has become an essential skill in this postpositivist, constructivist, and interconnected global society. Rather than taking the accuracy of new information for granted, students must learn to ask themselves if they are seeing events accurately and interpreting them through lenses that minimize distortion. Reflective discourse is the means by which we become aware of our lenses and learn to switch them for clear vision in changing circumstances (Mezirow & Associates, 2000). "Reflective discourse develops best when participants are well informed, free from coercion, listen attentively, have equal opportunities to participate and take a critical stance toward established cultural norms or viewpoints" (Belenky & Stanton, 2000, p. 71).

Although Mezirow and his colleagues (2000) may not have intended for their work to provide a foundation for justice-based critiques of society, it seems obvious that this approach implies a justice-oriented process. When participants in a discussion are expected to be free from coercion and take critical stances toward cultural norms, a process of criticizing injustice seems almost inevitable. This type of reflective discourse implies the development of cognitive complexity among the participants because multiple perspectives must be held in awareness and critiqued from multiple viewpoints. The notion of being free from coercion and listening attentively also evokes the notions of embodied learning, constructivism, and social intelligence (Goleman, 1998). By suggesting that learning is most powerful and transformative when it involves interpersonal communication, the simultaneous awareness of multiple points of view, respect for knowledge construction based on different and unequal life experiences, and a general sense of the context in which learning occurs, almost every assumption of traditional approaches to education is challenged.

Herbers describes the process of becoming aware of assumptions and lenses in four stages: "a) disorienting dilemmas, b) critical reflection, c) rational dialogue, and d) action" (as cited in Glisczinski, 2007, p. 320). He also cites the similarity between this cycle and Kolb's (1984) notion of experiential learning as a process of moving through concrete experience, reflection, abstract conceptualization, and active experimentation. Kolb's description has recently been affirmed by Zull (2002) as conforming to the methods and processes the brain uses to acquire, interpret, and apply new information during the learning process.

The ways we name experiences shape the learning process. If we have an experience we already have a name for, for example, red light means stay on the curb, little learning occurs because we are not disoriented. If we have an experience we don't have a name for, or our name seems inappropriate (e.g., Muslims are violent. Why is this imam telling me that Islam means peace?), we need to make sense of the new information and give it a new name. Names matter. Names indicate that entire paradigms are in operation and that they may or may not be providing guidance for understanding or taking action.

Why is this book called *Transformative Learning Through Engagement?* Names matter. I have been consistently puzzled by the contrast between the popularity of *Shifting Paradigms in Student Affairs* (Fried & Associates, 1995) and the apparently limited impact it has had on practice. Going back farther, both my students and I have been puzzled by the same response to *Student Personnel Work as Deeper Teaching* (Lloyd-Jones & Smith, 1954). My students immediately recognize that Lloyd-Jones and Smith were discussing experiential education and moral and cognitive development as aspects of student personnel work, even though those disciplines had not yet matured to their current prominence in the learning discourse.

The lineage of student personnel work/student affairs as a teaching/learning process is immediately recognizable as soon as the appropriate lens is used. Lloyd-Jones and Smith called it *deeper teaching,* a term that referred to educating students as whole people, teaching them to reflect on their own experiences as a means of developing the skills of democratic equality in interpersonal and community relationships. John Dewey (1916), who was a colleague of Lloyd-Jones at Columbia, also emphasized using the educational process to help students analyze and learn from their experience, equipping themselves to be effective citizens of a democracy. He discussed "the continuous reconstruction of experience [and] the enrichment of content or meaning of experiences" (as cited in Frankena, 1965, pp. 140–141). Dewey's (1938) purpose was to encourage the formation of habits and attitudes he described as "emotional and intellectual . . . basic sensitivities and ways of meeting and responding to all the conditions which we meet in living" (p. 35). Dewey considered all learning to have social and phenomenological components as well as external and objective components. In his paradigm, objective and internal conditions combined to create situations. Situations and interactions led to continuous learning and could not be separated from each other.

Dewey had a powerful impact on K–12 education but was not very influential in the pedagogy of higher education except through the work of Lloyd-Jones, whose contribution to student affairs was the emphasis on using experience as a teaching/learning tool. Her learning paradigm was embedded in experience and reflection. It did not conform to the positivist paradigm that has dominated higher education in the United States for more than a century, a paradigm that emphasizes information transfer, repetition, and application but not personal phenomenology or meaning making. Using the dominant framework of teaching and learning in American higher education, it is very difficult to perceive experience as a source of learning in an academic context. In positivist epistemology, academic credit is generally not associated with experiential learning that is inevitably constructivist. This paradigm of what constitutes learning and how learning can be documented is embedded in the consciousness of most people who work in higher education as the way things are. This paradigm is so powerful that it shapes our view of learning in ways we often do not see.

Learning Reconsidered (Keeling, 2004) has had a trajectory in the literature of student affairs similar to that of *Student Personnel Work as Deeper Teaching* (Lloyd-Jones & Smith, 1954). Lloyd-Jones's work, including her contribution to the *Student Personnel Point of View* (*SPPV*; American Council on Education [ACE], 1937), shaped the first modern generation of student personnel workers and student affairs administrators. Both versions of the *SPPV* (1937, 1949) made explicit discussions of educating the whole student and the critical role of this kind of education to the formation of competent citizens central to the work. *Learning Reconsidered* discusses civic engagement, inter- and intrapersonal competence, cognitive complexity and persistence, and academic achievement as central to the work of higher education.

Although the terminology has changed, the focus is very similar, and the lens is becoming clearer. The core work of the student affairs profession is to help students learn to live in a world with a sense of vocation, commitment to skillful participation in a democratic society, and the ability to live productively in family and community. Many of our academic colleagues share these values (Bok, 2006), and these aspirations also appear in the mission statements of many of our educational institutions. All of these skills and abilities require increasing cognitive complexity and the willingness to continue to learn new skills and information as circumstances demand. The ultimate goal is to help students create a sense of meaning and purpose for their lives that appreciates the individual in a community and global context (Parks, 2000).

This is noble work. Intellectual and professional competence, even brilliance, is far less meaningful and valuable to the human community than the capacity to hold these abilities in a context of meaning and value for those who use them and for those they are intended to serve. Quoting William Perry, Parks noted that

> the purpose of organisms is to organize and what human beings organize is meaning. Meaning making is the activity of composing a sense of the connections among things: a sense of pattern, order, form, and significance. To be human is to seek coherence and correspondence. . . . Patterning, testing, and recomposing activity occurs in every aspect of human life and manifests itself in meaning. (2000, p. 19)

What are the connections between the popularity of all the works cited here and the difficulty members of the student affairs profession have in framing the work we do with students as education and learning? Why do we continue to use the words *learning* and *development* as if they were two separate processes when we know that development supports learning cognitively and emotionally? I have come to believe that the problem lies in the positivist paradigm of learning and teaching that has shaped higher education in the Western world since the Industrial Revolution. Its roots can be traced to the lecture method of teaching that was in place at Oxford University before the invention of movable type. Books were few, and students learned by listening to faculty members share what they knew. Students demonstrated learning by repeating what faculty members said to them at designated times during the day and at the end of a course of study. If our paradigm of learning and teaching is positivist, based on the ability to remember and repeat information in a world where personal meaning is considered to distort accurate understanding, student affairs work will never be considered teaching, and the learning process that students undergo because of their work with us will not be considered legitimate learning that is comparable to legitimate academic learning. Within the positivist paradigm of information transfer and exclusion of personal meaning, student affairs work cannot be considered teaching in any meaningful sense. The paradigm of teaching/learning that has shaped higher education is blinding us to our own contributions to learning and making it extremely difficult to discuss our work as teaching. The current preoccupation with assessment of program effectiveness and with learning outcomes is one manifestation of our inability to understand how student affairs activities contribute to learning. We believe that if we can put numbers on a learning phenomenon, we can argue more effectively that learning has occurred. And we can argue more effectively if we demonstrate that our work with students has outcomes that can be documented. But these outcomes will generally not be considered learning in a legitimate, academic sense as long as we are operating in the positivist epistemological paradigm.

Barker (1992) describes this problem as one of physiological paradigm filters:

> Any data that exists in the real world that does not fit your paradigm will have a difficult time getting through your filters. . . . What we actually perceive is dramatically determined by our paradigms. What may be perfectly visible, perfectly obvious to persons with one paradigm, may be, quite literally, invisible to persons with a different paradigm. This is the paradigm effect. (p. 86)

A similar problem was documented on the basketball court when observers were told to watch the behavior of players who were wearing specific uniforms and to count passes. In their focus on player behavior, most of the observers missed the man on the floor in the gorilla suit who was wandering around on the court during the game (Chabris & Simons, 2009). Seeing is not believing. Believing is seeing. Our own paradigm of teaching and learning is making a more complete understanding of the educational work we do with students difficult to impossible. Names matter. Paradigms filter. It is truly time for a new paradigm of student affairs as teaching/learning based on the latest knowledge we have about what learning really means and how it really happens. One aspect of this paradigmatic transformation is to begin the integration of teaching and learning across the academic/student affairs border so that colleagues can develop transformative, integrated pedagogies.

Science and Learning

Until the development of functional magnetic resonance imaging (fMRI) there were few reliable methods for documenting learning processes except by observation of student behavior and reports by teachers and students about learning they had either observed or experienced. When Dewey (1938) developed pragmatist approaches to education he was reflecting on his own learning experiences and formalizing the process so that it could be used by others. He knew from personal experience and logical extrapolation the approaches to learning that would create skill, the capacity for continued learning, and most important, develop habits of mind and behavior that would permit students to continue to learn and live in democratic societies after their formal education was complete. Dewey did not separate learning from the set of skills and abilities we now call civic engagement.

When the second version of the *SPPV* was published in 1949, it was clear that the authors connected learning and democracy. They acknowledged the three traditional purposes of higher education, but they added new Deweyan dimensions in an effort to broaden the scope and role of higher education in the postwar world.

> The central purpose of higher education is the preservation, transmittal, and enrichment of culture by means of instruction, scholarly work, and scientific research. During the past few decades experience has pointed up the desirability of broadening this purpose to embrace additional emphases and objectives. Among these new goals, three stand out:
>
> 1. Education for a fuller realization of democracy in every phase of living;
> 2. Education directly and explicitly for international understanding and cooperation;
> 3. Education for the application of creative imagination and trained intelligence to the solution of social problems and to the administration of public affairs. (ACE, 1949, p. 108).

This work (ACE, 1949) explicitly acknowledged the contextual elements of learning and the role of student affairs in the experiential learning process. The authors asserted the importance of going beyond "German-born intellectualism" (p. 110) and recognizing the "psychology of individual differences" (p. 110) to shape the argument for what is now called constructivist learning. "It is axiomatic today that no man lives in a social vacuum. . . . [the individual] is constantly affecting society; and society is constantly shaping him" (p. 111). All students should be educated to hold an "enlightened belief in democracy" (p. 111) as part of their total educational experience in college. When the *SPPV* authors wrote about educating students to hold this belief, they were not talking about simply requiring everybody to take a course in American government or politics. Based on the pragmatist approach to learning, they expected students to learn to live and work in groups and to make decisions democratically, taking the welfare of other group members into account. The fact that John Dewey spent much of his youth in Vermont where town meetings are still the major venue for local decision making is no coincidence. He learned how to participate, the consequences of participation or nonparticipation, and the effect his views and participation had on his own welfare and the welfare of others in his town.

Dewey (1938), Lloyd-Jones (1954), and Crookston (1974), who was one of Lloyd-Jones' doctoral students, all understood and wrote about context, perspective, education for behavioral change, and citizenship. What they did not have available was language that would be accepted by those trained in the tradition of German-born intellectualism or to provide scientific evidence that a broader approach to learning might have more socially desirable consequences in a complex world where democracy could not be taken for granted. They also did not realize how difficult it is to provoke the types of paradigm shifts that would allow the educational establishment to change its view of learning. The old aphorism, "The most difficult thing in the world to change is your mind," turns out to be scientifically accurate.

The Physiology of Learning

The path information follows from sensation to perception/awareness to cognition is long and complex (Siegel, 2007). What Barker (1992) called *paradigm paralysis* or the *paradigm effect*, Siegel calls *top-down neural circuitry*. This web of brain circuits catalogs incoming data and files it in preestablished cognitive categories that are shaped by highly stable neural networks.

"On a practical level, if our past top-down influences create an internal set of 'shoulds,' then becoming enslaved by these beliefs without meta-awareness would make us prey to being quite judgmental about ourselves and others" (Siegel, p. 137). Siegel writes about self-awareness and learning new ways to think about self, but his ideas apply to learning how to think about almost anything. The overarching reason it is so hard to change our minds is that our minds are not the isolated, rational, intellectual processes we have been trained to believe they are. Our brains are embedded in our bodies, and our minds are a result of neurological, chemical, and electrical information transfer that enters our human experience as thoughts, feelings, actions, history, and the narrative of who we believe we are. A person simply cannot change his or her mind. What changes is everything from memory to biochemistry to feelings and relationships. Anyone who has tried to change any problem habit, like smoking, drinking alcohol, or eating junk food, knows how hard it is to change. Anyone who has moved away from a childhood home or moved to another country or changed jobs or attended college knows how hard it is to adapt. What we don't generally know about are the processes, most of them far below consciousness, that must activate to allow us to make these kinds of complex changes.

The Paradigm Challenge

I often remind my students that student development education as professional tradition is incredibly difficult to conceptualize. Until reading Siegel (2007), I was content to remark that we were overturning a 1,000-year-old-tradition, and that kind of change does not happen quickly. As a result of the writings of Siegel and his many colleagues, I have come to understand that changing a paradigm as vast and complex as the framework of higher education is far more difficult than I ever imagined. Changing our notions of teaching, learning, credibility, and validity involves far more than changing organizational structures, pedagogy, and administrative processes. All of us who are employed in higher education must rethink what we mean when we say *learning*; what we believe about objectivity, assessment, fairness, the connections between thinking and feeling; and what the goals of our institutions truly are. Most colleges have somewhere in their mission statements a comment about teaching citizenship that is not attached to any specific aspect of the curriculum. Student activities programs and residential life activities include learning about leadership, conflict management, self-awareness, interpersonal relationships, and a myriad of other attributes and skills that are prominent in the student affairs literature but almost invisible in traditional academic discussions of pedagogy. Students are not born knowing how to be citizens, and they are not born knowing how to solve problems, lead, set goals, or deal with ambiguous and uncomfortable circumstances. Yet the student affairs literature (Pascarella & Terenzini, 2005) reminds us that students do improve in all these areas between their arrival at college and their departure with degree in hand. Someplace in their college experience, students learn these skills or improve on the skill level they had on arrival.

Higher education as an institution, and as an archetype, manifests what Siegel (2007) calls enslavement to top-down neural network processing. This means we have highly developed neural information processing circuits in our brains that shape how we interpret what we see, hear, and learn. We are all victims of our preconceived ideas about everything until we learn not to be. Is something worth academic credit? How do we decide? What evaluative criteria do we use? Has somebody learned something because she or he created a student organization and carried out a year's worth of activities? How do we assign credit to this kind of holistic learning? This conflict about what we mean when we say *learning* happens almost every time a student affairs professional presents a course to an academic curriculum committee. The process is painful, unequal and often fruitless. Difficulties arise not because of malice but because of different ideas about the meaning of the term *learning* and the appropriateness of assigning academic credit. Our problem is a language problem and an epistemology problem. It is a problem of which lens is being used to interpret the phenomena and the failure of those in the conversation to make the lenses and their implied paradigms an explicit part of the conversation.

As a profession, we often do not engage in reflective conversations that explore the impact of the various lenses in use on the conversation. If student affairs professionals don't know what lens we are using, and equally important, if we don't understand the positivist lens that most academic faculty use when discussing learning, how can we make progress? Student affairs professionals are as much enslaved in the positivist perspective as are our academic colleagues. After all, we are college graduates, and we learned about academic learning from people very similar to those who are now our colleagues at our own institution. We know students learn because of our work with them. We can hear it in the way they explain their views and see it in their changed behavior as they become more experienced. But we often lack the language to explain these changes in terms of learning to our academic colleagues, much less explain why this kind of learning, which is heavily experiential, ought to be part of the accredited learning processes of the institution.

If those of us in the student affairs profession want to be acknowledged as full participants in the learning processes of our institutions, we must begin by looking at our own paradigms and learning how to talk about them. We must be able to explain why our work with students is as much a teaching/learning process as is the work of our academic colleagues. We need the language, and we need a minimal understanding of learning as revealed in fMRI research. Most of all we need to reflect on our own preconceived ideas about the nature of our work—what we do, how we do it, how it has changed in the past 50 years, and what the learning needs of our current students seem to be. The student affairs profession is based on constructivist epistemology. We know there is never one point of view that explains everything. We know that in some cases no one will ever know the truth about what really happened in a roommate conflict. But we also know that if people talk to each other, significant, transformative learning is possible whether you can take a test about it or not.

I do believe the hardest thing in the world to change is your mind. Now I know why mind changing is so difficult. And I also know that no matter how many workshops we attend, the paradigm about learning in college will not shift until every one of us learns to change her or his mind, acknowledges that in paradigm shifts everybody goes back to zero (Barker, 1992), and that we all find ways to talk about this challenge with each other.

3

SEARCHING FOR CLARITY

A butterfly is not just a caterpillar who grows
wings. Becoming a butterfly requires total transformation, dissolving and reforming.

—Anonymous

In order to create a truly multicultural organization, we must start from scratch. Organizations
that already exist must be disbanded. There is
no way to add people of color after the fact and
still create a multicultural organization.

—Angela Davis, 1989

White graduate student to professor: I need to do some reading really fast. I've been working with all White students but now I've got a job where the students are mostly minorities. Professor: Then that makes you a minority. Student: Silence. (J. Fried, personal conversation, 1994)

Why do we as student affairs professionals need to understand experiential learning, meaning making, and diversity of all kinds? On the surface, this seems like a question with some obvious answers. Experiential education constitutes a great deal of what we do with students. Almost everything we do that affects students has some potential to become a learning experience or to shape a learning opportunity. Every meeting, training program, career counseling or academic advising session, or disciplinary conversation has the potential to help students learn. Our students have become incredibly diverse in their characteristics and their learning needs.

In the late 20th century, higher education struggled with the issues provoked by cultural diversity—access, remediation, understanding across cultures, different norms for different groups, and valuing the contributions of each group to the campus community. In the 21st century, issues of diversity have extended to multiracial students (Literte, 2010) as well as to students with a range of disabilities including learning, psychological, and physical. The latest arrivals on campus are returning veterans, many of whom have war-related injuries including post-traumatic stress disorder, brain damage, and physical disabilities. In addition, our understanding of gender, sex role socialization, and the fluidity of gender identity (Abes, Jones, & McEwan, 2007) has become far more complex as "queer" students demand our understanding and support. Because of the retirement of many baby boomer faculty members, we are also seeing our new faculty colleagues manifest a similar range of diverse identities and conditions, all of which require us to develop new skills.

The current state of cultural complexity on our campuses reflects circumstances in the wider society. Gay, lesbian, and transgender people demand civil rights protections equal to those of all other citizens. Citizens with disabilities expect that services and supports will be provided so they can participate in society on an equal basis with others. Immigration, legal and illegal, is at the highest level in our history. California no longer has a majority ethnic group. Women continue to experience pay inequity and other unsanctioned forms of discrimination, but there are few remaining legal barriers to work opportunities in any field. The scope of diverse interactions that occur in daily life on our campuses demands a new level of skill to make communication and understanding possible (Pope, Reynolds, & Mueller, 2004).

All these challenging situations provide additional opportunities for learning, and most of these opportunities do not occur in classrooms. Nevertheless, these opportunities fall within the educational paradigm described for the student affairs profession in *A Student Personnel Program for Higher Education* (Lloyd-Jones & Smith, 1938) and expanded in the first and second edition of *The Student Personnel Point of View* (ACE, 1937, 1949). The skills and abilities described in *Learning Reconsidered* (Keeling, 2004) continue this trend of describing the work of student affairs as experiential education intended to teach students how to live successfully in a complex society. If these conditions are currently shaping campuses in the United States, and most of these campuses employ student affairs professionals in a range of different kinds of roles, why does the conversation about the educational work of the student affairs profession remain problematic? The search for answers to this question involves an analysis of American values and thought processes that go back to the founding of this country and tend to remain obscure to this day.

Worldviews Shaped by Science and History

The United States is in the midst of a profound transformation that is shifting our fundamental view of reality. This paradigm shift affects our "basic ways of perceiving, thinking, valuing, and doing" (Harman, 1988, p. 10). The last comparable shift occurred in Europe during the Age of Enlightenment, when notions of fundamental reality and reliable knowledge shifted from faith to reason. Truth came to be identified with corroboration through empirical data rather than wisdom or revelation (Harman; West, 1993b). Science came to dominate religion as the perspective that shaped credible understanding of life and world events. Medieval science, with its goal of understanding Divine purpose and meaning, was transformed into modern science with its goal of description, prediction, and control (Capra, 1982). The change took at least 300 years to pervade popular thought, beginning in the Renaissance (mid-16th century) and becoming dominant during the Industrial Revolution (late 19th century).

Because the scientific, materialistic way of perceiving and understanding the world has become so totally pervasive in American culture, we are generally not aware of the ways it shapes our view of events. Historically, science has assumed there is an absolute separation between the observer and the observed. This principle of scientific methodology began to become obsolete with Heisenberg's notion that "you cannot observe a particle without disturbing it," but the general conception of scientific neutrality and the irrelevance of viewpoint continues to shape the public perception (Hawley & Uretsky, 2011). In our common understanding the scientist examines data to discover inherent patterns that can then serve as categories upon which future analyses are conducted and future events predicted. The process of creating categories involves sorting out complex phenomena into relatively discrete groups. All reliable data are empirical, that is, able to be observed and measured or described with regard to their physical characteristics or behavior. Since categories are assumed to be discovered in the data rather than created by the observer, the role of human perception, assumptions, or values in this process is typically minimized or denied.

In our daily lives, we create categories all the time. This is an essential skill for children to learn early in life (Kegan, 2000). It helps them to communicate with others and to understand culturally and contextually appropriate behavior. For example, children learn that any object one sits on can be called a chair. These objects are distinct from other objects we recline on, called beds, or objects we stand on, called stools. Kegan refers to these basic concepts as *durable categories.* The ability to form durable categories permits us to create social perceptions and to understand the notion of point of view. These are foundational elements of epistemology that ultimately enable people to live in groups and understand culture by creating meaning and reflect or revise previously created meanings (Kegan).

Initially, these categories seem natural and universal. Beyond simple categories of use, some types of beds, stools, or chairs may also be considered better, fancier, or more worth having than others. The determination of what seems better is not an objective process but rather one based on cultural values or personal preferences. Durable categories evolve into the capacity for transcategorical comparisons (Kegan, 2000), and these comparisons tend to cluster into personal or cultural lenses through which individuals make sense of the world. Our lenses or categories of perception tend to enhance certain similarities and differences and ignore others. The lenses themselves are shaped by the language and attitudes of the people who care for us as we are learning to describe the world in early childhood. For example, what is the significant difference between a low table and a stool? Who determines the categories of stool versus table? The process of lens and category creation that appears so natural and inevitable to its users is a political as well as a linguistic process, fraught with value judgments and powerful in its ability to shape attitudes and behavior. It is generally acceptable to stand on a stool but not on a table.

People can also be sorted into categories. American culture seems particularly prone to this kind of category creation. For example, think of box checking on the federal census: What are you? White, Asian American, African American, non-White Hispanic, other? "What are you?" is a question people ask each other when they cannot determine ethnicity or race simply by looking at a person. What are you? You appear browner than a person of European descent and your accent when you speak English is different from the accents of White Americans who learned to speak in Nebraska. Categories that describe race or skin color are particularly salient in the United

States, and categorization by race has enormous political, social, and economic consequences.

The infinite number of categories we use to make sense of our complex life experiences are created by processes that combine observation of empirical data and value judgments about the data. Many categories Americans structure their lives by appear natural and objective to us and yet might appear quite bizarre or distorted to people from other cultures. Our commitment to separation of church and state is one such set of categories. Many Arab countries are governed or heavily influenced by Sharia law under which this separation of God's will from laws and public expectations is inconceivable and blasphemous. The State of Israel constantly struggles to balance demands by Orthodox Jews that its laws conform to the dictates of Torah and Halakah and the secular nature of its democracy. Both cultures create categories according to their own beliefs. These categories are dramatically challenged by the upheavals in several Middle Eastern countries in 2011. Those in the social sciences have created their analytic categories by using approaches that are similar to those used in the physical and biological sciences. However, social scientists have had more difficulty discovering sharp, clear categories that are relevant and significant for the issues they study than their colleagues in the natural sciences have.

When methods of scientific observation are used to study human behavior, people are considered fundamentally no different from atomic particles or other groups of phenomena whose activities can be understood through the lens of statistical analysis. Therefore, all observations of any given event should be quite similar. Categories and factual descriptions should be uniform across observers. This approach tends to break down when describing social phenomena in field sites rather than physical phenomena in laboratories. "One comes away from accounts of such research somewhat skeptical of its ultimate value as a source of deep understanding of human behavior" (Ziman, 1978, p. 167). Although it is possible to control the effects of perception and values in observation of physical phenomena, such control is almost impossible in category creation used to describe social phenomena. Many spiritual leaders and physicists have criticized the domination of what they call *scientism*, the assumption that scientific ways of knowing are sufficient to help human beings understand all domains of the human experience.

Scientism is the worldview held by a majority of people in the Western world that claims that all that "is" and all that "can be known" is verifiable or falsifiable through the scientific method, and that which cannot be so measured is simply opinion, belief, or fantasy. It cannot be known and sensibly talked about and hence should be relegated to the private sphere. (*Specter of Scientism*, 2007).

Historically, category creation around gender characteristics follows a similar pattern. Women have been presumed to be naturally more prone to developing nurturing relationships, becoming nurses, and doing social welfare work, while men are naturally more achievement oriented, competitive and autonomous, and prone to work with objects that can be manipulated. Carol Gilligan (1982), one of the first people who began to research characteristics of female moral development, was criticized as an essentialist because she actually asserted that women do think differently from men. Her findings were based on valid qualitative methodology but did not acknowledge there is always more within group variation than between group variation. Many men do make decisions on an ethic of caring, while many women use a justice orientation for the same purpose. Yet the essential distinction in the public mind between male and female characteristics persists.

Race also remains a very important category of distinction in the United States. Race is defined as including skin color and a range of other physical features. Race is presumed to be associated with culture, but this is not necessarily accurate and is often misleading. "The terms culture, ethnicity and race are often used interchangeably. Neither culture nor ethnicity necessarily has anything to do with race as the term is typically used in U.S. society or psychology" (Helms, 1994, pp. 291–292). When we say race is a problem, we are using an undefined term that causes a great deal of controversy, and we tend not to explain why it is a problem or for whom. Race is an accepted category of analysis. Once we accept the category, we lose sight of the social process that created the category. Americans tend to act as if we discovered the phenomenon of race, observed it without lenses, and made no judgments about it. We believe, because of the assumptions embedded in science, that *it* is simply there. A society could conceivably exist in which skin color/race was not a significant category, and social class serves as the important categories for sorting people into groups. Biologically, race is an illusion. Anthropologically and politically, racism is a fact of American life.

In the same fashion many faculty members believe their ideas about education are correct ideas or the only valid ideas and that people who play nonteaching roles are not part of the educational process. This is not to suggest that the noneducational status ascribed to student affairs professionals is as severe a problem on our campuses as racism. However, the difference in power and influence between student affairs professionals and academicians flows from a similar element of the American paradigm, the belief that categories exist a priori, and that people fit data into them rather than vice versa. Knowledge gleaned from books and laboratory experiments is considered more valuable than knowledge gleaned from holding a leadership role and taking about what is learned with an adviser or peers. The classic question curriculum committee members put to student affairs professionals when they seek acknowledgment of their educational work with students is, "Why should we award academic credit for this?" It is a question that often strikes articulate people dumb (Barr & Fried, 1981). The category of academic credit in relation to learning is so well defined in our minds, that even we, the members of a profession that constantly helps students learn, often cannot answer it.

Our definition of a category of analysis named *academic credit* is slowly beginning to change, and much of the content of this book is an effort to support and push the change process along. Both volumes of *Learning Reconsidered* (Keeling, 2004, 2006) constituted an effort to redefine learning to include cognition, affect, and behavior by incorporating experiential learning on and off campus into the overall discussion of student learning. The national movement to focus on student learning and assessing learning outcomes supports this type of category reframing. However, this process is slow and difficult because it is so complex. To reframe our understanding of learning and redefine the kinds of learning that deserve academic credit, educators and administrators need to become familiar with brain-based approaches (Johnson & Taylor, 2006), which are based on the physiology of learning, not on historical practice that dates from the Middle Ages. The notion of academic disciplines and the departmental structure that supports disciplines will need to be reexamined. Entire university administrative structures will need to be reshaped. Considering the scope of the project and numbers of people and institutions involved, this change will probably not happen quickly.

The scientific paradigm that has dominated American and Western thinking is characterized by rationality, materialism, objectivity, and belief in linear cause/effect change. The emerging paradigm emphasizes dynamic, complex interrelationships between people and events, mutual shaping, context, and an awareness of spirituality as an important aspect of human life (Capra, 1982; Gardner, 1995; Lazlo, 2008). The shift has been provoked by increasing intercultural communication and the rapid rate of technological change speeding up communication in all aspects of business, politics, and education. In the earlier paradigm, the change process might be compared to a game of billiards in which one action provokes another in a linear progression. In the second paradigm, one event can cause any number of consequences that then set other events in motion in apparently random order, often with unpredictable results (Wheatley, 1999). This type of change has been compared to shaking a web. Events in one part of the web may cause minor changes nearby but may be amplified throughout the system and have major consequences in unanticipated locations.

Because of the rapidity of the current change as well as transformations in global communication, our society is profoundly aware of the shift even when we cannot articulate our awareness beyond a felt sense of fear or anger. This awareness leads to greater visibility of the assumptions that shaped the old paradigm if only because so many are so uncomfortable with the loss of certainty these changes and the emerging paradigm provoke. The economic crises of the early 21st century have led to anger, frustration, and confusion in the general public while everybody waits for things to get back to normal. There seems to be little understanding that most political leaders and economists are in uncharted territory, searching for new frameworks to use in understanding and addressing problems. Although they can make reassuring statements to the public, the reality is that their own sense of certainty and what actions may improve public welfare are equally challenged. Terrorism is another phenomenon that sheds light on an outmoded paradigm. How does a country wage war on small groups of people who come from many countries and are motivated by their rendition of faith rather than patriotism? The entire landscape of international relations has been changed by this new form of violence.

On campus many paradigms operate simultaneously because students, faculty, and staff come from so many different cultures, faith perspectives, life experiences, developmental stages, and academic disciplines. The nondominant paradigms are often invisible or difficult to perceive because the scientific paradigm dominates most discussions and interpretations of events.

On the administrative side of the enterprise, empiricism appears as a preoc-cupation with the financial aspects of the institution and a general disregard for unmeasurable aspects of managing and learning (Readings, 1996; Tuch-man, 2009). In what some now describe as these difficult economic times, preoccupation with finances and organizational arrangements is understand-able, perhaps even commendable. However, this is a lens to view events, a set of constructed categories, not the only way to organize the institution or describe the process of learning.

Paradigms That Shape Our Vision

A societal or dominant paradigm is often compared to a set of lenses. Anyone who has ever received a prescription for a new set of eyeglasses or lenses is familiar with the experience of adjusting to the new vision. One becomes used to slightly blurred vision because of familiarity with one's daily terrain. New lenses bring new clarity, changing focus, a new sense of perspective and awareness. One is most acutely aware of the role lenses play at the time when lenses change. We are now changing lenses. We can still get along with the old ones, but they distort, confuse, and mislead under certain circumstances. However, they also provide a sense of comfort because of their familiarity. The comments by the White student at the beginning of this chapter who could not imagine himself as a minority person illustrates this problem. His construction of minority status is based on race or skin color. He assumes that light skin color from his European ancestry makes him a member of the majority no matter what the context. His ability to see the complexity of current life is based on a narrow lens he is unaware of. To understand how our American lens shapes our views of the world, it is helpful to know how and under what circumstances the lens was created. This process began in the New World at the time the original 13 English colonies were founded.

Roots

American culture uses a "pattern of opposed dualities" (Merelman, 1984, p. 22) in establishing acceptable beliefs and behaviors, determining who's in and who's out. This pattern is the social equivalent of two-valued logic used in science. Who hasn't seen "America—Love it or leave it" on a bumper sticker? The message behind "Love it" can easily be interpreted to mean "Act like the dominant group," or "Blend into the melting pot." American culture has been nominally assimilationist since its founding, but successful assimilation has been compared to committing cultural suicide for those whose home culture is significantly different from their adopted culture (Phelan, Davidson, & Hanh, 1993). Those whose values and behaviors are most similar to the dominant culture are most welcome. Muslims who wear traditional modest garb have had a great deal of difficulty assimilating and have had to take very assertive action to identify places in schools where they can pray at the appropriate times during the day. Americans have developed a cultural system and set of behavioral expectations to make sense of their world and to live with each other. This culture depends on a pattern of opposed dualities and helps Americans determine who is one of us and who is not. Almost anyone can be treated as one of us if she or he adopts the expected behaviors and can expect to be treated with suspicion if he or she does not.

Beyond certain boundaries, diversity is generally construed as messy, disorderly, ignorant, or unpatriotic. Conforming to American cultural codes permits immigrants and members of nondominant groups to assimilate. African American teenagers are often considered extremely noisy because the level of their social discourse exceeds the decibel level that sounds normal to most White people. Men who come to the United States from Mediterranean countries quickly learn not to embrace or kiss each other on the street because many Americans categorize them as gay and are uncomfortable with this public display of affection. People who come from cultures that encourage large families, early marriage, and emphasis on loyalty do not fit easily into the current American norm of small families, later marriage, and individual autonomy. Many American living spaces do not provide sufficient room for these extended families. Attempts to squeeze a family of five siblings, two parents, an uncle, and a grandmother into an affordable apartment may be considered evidence of squalid living and irresponsibility in family and economic planning.

American Norms and Values

The dominant culture in the United States, to the degree that it still exists, emphasizes the following characteristics and behavior: (a) high value on emotional control, individual autonomy, and achievements; (b) the written word over the spoken word; (c) youth over age; and (d) an emphasis on the future rather than the past or present (Ivey, Ivey, & Simek-Morgan, 1993). It also supports (e) the right of humans to dominate nature (Ibrahim, 1991) and (f) monotheistic religions that are intolerant of what they see as competing perspectives (Armstrong, 1993). The culture assumes that these values are normal and Americans rarely question or challenge them.

Reason and Intellect

Our intellectual inheritance is also derived from the European Enlightenment. This period was characterized by increasing faith in humans' ability to understand how the universe worked. Mystery became less important than logic and data. Galileo, whose work preceded the Enlightenment and made subsequent development possible, believed that truth could be expressed mathematically and that the entire physical universe could be described in quantifiable terms (Capra, 1982). Pascal, an Enlightenment philosopher, tried to find God through the use of reason and failed in despair. The new system of meaning making that swept Europe did not permit him to maintain a faith-centered personal universe. Charles Darwin had a similar problem and waited several years to publish his theory of evolution because of the implications of his findings for the Christian faith (Heiligman, 2009). Other thinkers adapted the empirical scientific method to investigate the material world and the world of faith. Descartes compared God's laws to the laws of geometry and asserted that any God who could produce perfect geometric laws could also be assumed to produce perfect laws to govern the rest of the world. The mechanical laws, once established, did not require any Divine intervention. People who adopted this belief system, including the founders of the United States, were called Deists. They affirmed a belief in God but assumed that the universe had been set in motion and would continue to run mechanically without further intrusion. People were seen as self-governing, thinking beings who could survive independently and understand the world by use of reason, logic, and experimentation. Isaac Newton compared God to a mechanic, and his self-chosen task was to discover God's physical laws so people could more accurately predict and control the physical world.

Enlightenment thinkers downplayed the role of emotions in their search for universal principles. They considered irregularities in data as anomalies that were confusing, misleading, or temporary. Anomalies were expected to disappear when a sufficiently general explanation for a phenomenon was discovered. These thinkers functioned in a relatively homogeneous intellectual environment with minimal exposure to Semitic, Asian, or African ideas. They extended the search for scientific truth to other aspects of the human experience, assuming that this application of science was viable and accurate. In early psychological studies of human development, for example, women were considered anomalies whenever their attributes seemed to differ from those of men (Gilligan, 1982). In studies of identity formation among gay men (D'Augelli, 1991), Latino/Latina students (Torres, 2003), and other students with multiple dimensions of identity (Abes & Jones, 2004; Abes, Jones, & McEwan, 2007), differences from the original linear development models are now studied seriously and assumed to have equal validity for the groups they describe.

Faith

Historically, our attitude toward religion has been tolerant of variations in monotheism but not other traditions and practices. Since September 11, 2001, relationships between Muslim Americans and immigrants who are of the faith of Islam have been seriously disrupted by terrorism and fear. American familiarity with Jewish and Christian monotheism has not extended to a similar comfort level with the third Abramic faith, nor does it extend to other religious practices and beliefs. All Abramic faiths officially reject the beliefs of nontheistic systems like Buddhism as well as polytheism and pantheism, which are practiced all over the world. The Bible of Christians and Jews instructs people to subdue the earth and have dominion over it, not to live in harmony with other forms of life and to respect them. This belief has shaped American behavior throughout our national history as we have dominated indigenous cultures within our borders, assimilated members of other immigrant ethnic groups, and Americanized countries we have occupied for economic or security reasons (Takaki, 2008). Our reliance on a belief in one God exemplifies the Enlightenment belief that the best explanation for anything is the one that explains the most details in a single theoretical framework.

Democracy and Individualism

Liberal democracy shapes American government and provides the next overlay in our cultural value system. Liberal democracies emphasize self-expression and self-development as the primary goals of government. The purpose of government is to maximize opportunities for the individual while maintaining some type of social contract that acknowledges the needs of the group (Margolis, 1979). This form of democracy enhances our beliefs in autonomy, achievement, emphasis on the future, and the virtues of youth as a source of energy and ideas. These democracies tend to focus on enhancing the freedom of individuals to do what they wish and to focus on meeting the needs of communities only when forced to do so. Liberal democracies have been considered very effective at preserving the rights of free speech, fairness in legal and judicial processes, tolerating differences, and guaranteeing that no group will be totally excluded from the system (Merelman, 1984). However, they are considered less effective in building trust between groups that have different values and behavior patterns or establishing a consensus under any but the most serious of circumstances such as in times of war (Merelman). This problem appears constantly in the form of conflicts between conservationists and land developers, supporters of social welfare systems and supporters of free enterprise and rugged individualism, and supporters of globalization of economic activity versus supporters of keeping more economic activity within U.S. borders. Conflicts over First Amendment rights also fall into this category, particularly free speech versus hate speech. Because of the emphasis on individuality and autonomy, citizens of liberal democracies are often unaware of social contexts and cultural values that shape individuals (Merelman). This makes it difficult for many Americans to differentiate between cultural and personal differences.

The emphasis on individualism in American culture is considered extreme by many social critics (Bellah, Madsen, Sullivan, Swidler, & Tipton, 1985; Lasch, 1979; Young, 1990). Our historical concern with the rights of the individual over the welfare of the community has been exacerbated by events that make it difficult to separate the two. These kinds of conflicts include difficulty in controlling our borders (Who has the right to be here?); Internet harassment (freedom of speech?); the interconnection of global economics (free enterprise?); and the obvious connections among all aspects of our environment pointed out whenever a tsunami, earthquake, or other environmental disaster occurs. Given our emphasis on individualism and our preoccupation with finding unified explanations, most Americans do not have a mental map to help them make their way in this confusion and social fragmentation. Our national identity has been based on the belief in a unified American culture. Yet, "By 2056 most Americans will trace their descent to Africa, Asia, the Hispanic world, the Pacific Islands, Arabia and other parts of the middle east—almost anywhere but white Europe" (Takaki, 2008, p. 2). The national identity described in many of our history books has become inaccurate and misleading. It is currently impeding our ability to function as a multicultural internally cohesive society because the metaphor and myth ignores and excludes members of many nondominant groups, most obviously those who trace their roots to places other than Europe.

Consequences for Student Affairs and Higher Education

Why do we as student affairs professionals need to understand cultural complexity? The vast majority of student affairs professionals are cultural or acculturated Americans. The student affairs profession is built on a group of categories that reflect the value system described previously. Ours is a fairly narrow lens. It focuses on a future narrowly defined as an extension of the present but tends not to imagine divergent human experiences, particularly those shaped by other cultures. Many Americans have trouble seeing or understanding culture because we generally lack a point of comparison. We experience our own culture as a singular reality because it is the only reality we experience on a day-to-day basis.

Those who exemplify the dominant culture most thoroughly (White, Anglo Saxon, Christian, heterosexual, able bodied, male) are generally the ones facing the greatest challenge to learn to see with new lenses. Those who lack one or more aspects of the dominant heritage have probably been forced into an awareness of lenses sometime during their lives. Jews know about Christians because they cannot avoid the contrast, particularly during the Christmas and Easter seasons. Americans of color know about Americans of European ancestry because they dominate the media and all the major institutions in the country and currently outnumber them. Until the past 30 years or so one could not tell from advertisements that people of color in the United States brushed their teeth, smoked, washed clothes, or ate at fast-food restaurants. People of color cannot avoid seeing the contrasts between themselves and members of the dominant culture because they cross the border between cultures daily. The same comparisons have applied to the lesbian, gay, bisexual, and transgender population, although representations of this group are also becoming more visible in the media.

Americans who see the world through a monocultural lens may not be conceptually or emotionally prepared to accept the current range of differences of appearance, belief, and behavior as normal. Diversity may appear confusing, frustrating, or simply uncomfortable. Many Americans haven't learned to think that difference is valuable or worth understanding because we are simply waiting for it to go away, to be able to think of all people as "just human beings," without defining what that means or what it ignores. Diversity makes us afraid of interacting with others. We don't know what members of other groups expect of us, how they want to be treated, what offends them, or why in some instances they act the way they do. We are biologically predispositioned to bond with people we define as us and to fear or avoid people who are different. These predispositions are generally unconscious but are typically more powerful than anything in our relationships that we are aware of (R. Hanson, personal communication, January 7, 2011). As student affairs professionals, we have put ourselves through thousands of diversity workshops in an effort to understand differences. White Americans have asked our colleagues of color to explain their experiences to us ad nauseam, until many of them have given up in frustration. In an even more sensitive area, heterosexual student affairs professionals have pushed themselves to understand their gay and lesbian colleagues and have experienced a great deal of discomfort in facing the fluidity of their own sexuality. We do not have a comprehensive picture of the effectiveness of these approaches, but we continue to engage in them regardless.

To summarize, Americans of the dominant culture have difficulty in understanding, perceiving, experiencing, and valuing differences among people because

- we are not used to thinking that significant differences among people are normal;
- we don't have a cultural perspective that values difference;
- we work in bureaucracies originally designed to carry out standardized tasks with and for people with essentially similar needs, and diversity in this framework is a problem by definition; and
- we are unaware of many elements in our own culture and therefore have trouble knowing when our discomfort is related to the crossing of our taken for granted cultural borders such as interpersonal space, noise levels, and eye contact. We also have trouble distinguishing between differences shaped by culture and those influenced by individual personality.

Engaging with significant differences for most Americans is profoundly disorienting. It challenges our sense of self, our national values, our faith, and our ways of making sense of the world. It forces us to reexamine our most deeply held beliefs and perhaps our hidden behaviors as well. We are asked to do this in a culture that believes there is a right or best way to do everything. Therefore we may find things in ourselves we don't like, believe are wrong, or provoke shame. Engaging with significant difference is frightening emotionally and challenging intellectually. A person cannot remain at the lower levels of any scale of cognitive development and truly understand diversity. Any effort to dismantle the mental architecture that makes novelty frightening and enslaves us to rigid, preconceived notions about people or events is experienced as a threat to our own continued existence (Siegel, 2007).

Experiencing a world in which diverse perspectives and cultures coexist is frightening and disorienting. If one is used to living in a world of hierarchical values and unitary ideas about goodness, diversity throws everything into disarray. How will we know how to act, what is right, whom to appreciate? If our lifestyle contains hidden elements that were previously devalued and might be revealed, such as sexual orientation, chronic dependency on people or substances, or chronic disease or disability, how will we know what is safe to reveal and under what circumstances? We will have to rethink everything. Asking Americans of the dominant culture to accept diversity is almost as difficult as asking medieval Christians to accept a world where the sun, not God or the earth, is at the center. When we began to talk abut Affirmative Action, we really didn't know where the road would take us. We didn't know the cost of assimilation for so many members of nondominant groups. And we certainly didn't know that at some point members of these groups would no longer be willing to pay the admission prices of cultural self-destruction (Cose, 1993).

Moving Toward Multiple Lenses

Anyone who has studied theories of cognitive development is familiar with the standard, linear, sequential approach these theories use. Individuals begin thinking at a binary or dualistic level in which the world is divided into black and white, and authority is external and absolute (Perry, 1968). They progress toward more complex views of the world until they reach a stage where there is no longer a sense of external authority, right answers, or absolute truth. There are hypotheses and commitments that permit a person to make good choices, use available evidence, and learn to manage the ambiguity that comes with living in an uncertain world (King & Kitchener, 1994).

We are now at a point where our profession and ultimately significant numbers of cultural Americans must move along these scales to the place where they can understand multiple perspectives, make justifiable but tentative commitments, and learn to live with the insecurity of ambiguity. We can see these changes occurring in our political and economic life right now. The United States is still the most powerful economy in the world, but Brazil, China, and India are moving up quickly. We cannot dictate events in the Middle East or Afghanistan regardless of how much we want cheap oil or the end of terrorism. We must collaborate everywhere to advance our own national agenda. We cannot rescue our own economy unless the economies of our trading partners are also improving. And even if sports fans are still fond of waving foam rubber signs that indicate their team is number one, the signs indicating that the United States is number one are rapidly diminishing (Zakaria, 2008). We need a new model for relating to other countries, and we need a new model for thinking about how to help students learn what matters in their lives. We need to construct new categories and see through new lenses.

4

BELIEVING IS SEEING

American Cultural Norms

T he old adage "Seeing is believing" has been turned upside down. We now know that believing has a huge impact on what we see and, more importantly, on how we interpret information. Research on learning and memory (Siegel, 2007; Zull, 2006) has clarified the neurochemical processes used by the brain to perceive, acquire, retain, catalog, and connect new information in a way that is far more complicated than was previously understood. The complex belief system American civilization is built on was outlined in the previous chapter. Now it is time to examine how belief systems are learned and what might be involved if we want to do some significant deconstruction of our beliefs to bring traditional perspectives into line with current demands.

The "four fundamental pillars" of learning are "gathering, reflecting, creating, and testing" (Zull, 2006, p. 5). As we perceive new information, the brain catalogs it in different locations that are specialized for seeing, hearing, remembering, feeling, and other functions. Gathering new information has historically been synonymous with most conceptions of learning, but gathering is only the first part of the process. As the information is perceived, it is compared to memories of similar situations and deposited in a bank of memories that move from short term to long term as connections are made. If new information does not match well with preconceived ideas, the brain smoothes out the differences and creates new more coherent memories. The entire process is neurochemical and time consuming. Brains develop maps of neural circuits that operate as filing systems, and these filing systems determine where new information is likely to be placed and how it will be evaluated and used. For example, if *Jewish* has been filed in association with *unsaved* in a person's brain, that person might be more likely to approach a Jewish person with evangelizing in mind than a person who files *Jewish* along with *bagels*, or some other more neutral term.

These filing systems create dynamic processes of information storage and exchange in the brain that affect every bit of new data that are placed into meaning-making systems that allow people to live without stopping to question every thought and action. These powerful neurological filing systems are what Siegel (2007) described as "enslavement" (p. 135). This term signifies the distorting power of preconceived ideas or neural connections. New data that conflict with preconceived ideas create problems in the meaning-making system because they do not fit into preestablished categories. This discomfort has been labeled *cognitive dissonance*, and most of us are quite familiar with experiencing this kind of distress. Sometimes seeing, especially if we see what is there and don't get caught in seeing what we thought would be there, is disbelieving. British singer Susan Boyle's first performance on a television talent show provoked enormous cognitive dissonance because her appearance simply did not match her vocal performance, and she strained the neural circuitry of the judges and millions of viewers.

New insights tend to occur after a period of reflection, much of which is not conscious. In fact, the process of sleeping on it or taking time out before making a decision relies on the time it takes for connections to be made neurochemically as values, beliefs, and memories are patched together. Reflection is the conscious part of the process of making connections, but the connections may occur chemically with no conscious awareness until the light goes on and understanding emerges. In fact, reflection can be supplemented by mindful meditation because the connective processes rely largely on a lack of turbulence in brain function (Hanson, 2009). After the brain integrates the new information, action processes begin, deciding what to do with the information. This process involves verbal and visual imagery and occurs in the frontal cortex, where it provides the "basis for conscious thought and planning," which Zull (2006) calls "the most elevated aspect of learning . . . required for the development of deep understanding" (p. 6). Finally, the learner tests the efficacy of the new idea, and the learning cycle continues.

Surrounding the filing and interpreting process is a bath of chemicals that carry emotions and whose significance cannot be overstated. Emotions have an impact on the signal processes of the filing system and affect every element of learning. "Emotion is the foundation of learning. The chemicals of emotion act by modifying the strength and contribution of each part of the learning cycle" (Zull, 2006, p. 7). Descartes had some powerful insights about the role of reason in human life when he declared, "I think, therefore I am." Unfortunately, he was unaware of the role emotion plays in learning. The architecture of many universities and colleges has become a metaphor of Descartes' insight. The role of student affairs in the learning process has been limited by the Cartesian framework that privileges thinking over experience and emotion.

We now realize that human beings learn in an integrated fashion. Any attempt to divide thinking from feeling, acting, and integrating learning with living is bound to produce less powerful learning than learning which integrates Zull's (2006) four pillars. We also know that an enormous amount of learning occurs before students arrive at college, and much of that learning has come from living in families and communities. Students continue to learn in college from the events of their daily lives on and off campus by acquiring new information, reflecting on it, placing it in their own neural filing systems, and acting on old or new insights about behavior required for success.

The Historic American Cultural Framework

The title of this chapter, "Believing Is Seeing," gives rise to several very important questions from the new perspective that believing shapes seeing rather than vice versa. What have students who were raised in the United States come to believe about the way the world works for them? How do these beliefs affect their learning, their relationships with others, and their overall ability to succeed in college? How does the dominant American cultural paradigm shape their lenses for interpreting the world? What are the traditional elements of this paradigm or lens and how does it affect the ability to do well on campuses where students from many cultures study and faculty from many cultures teach? If emotions are the foundation of learning, and students are challenged by strong emotions such as fear, enthusiasm, sex drive, anxiety, and depression on a daily basis (Chickering & Reisser, 1993), how do these emotions affect their ability to learn or shape what they learn? Is the dominant American paradigm that provides the neural map students use to interpret the world inhibiting or supporting their growth? If learning is inhibited by their neural architecture we must ask ourselves how to create a learning process in which emotions are considered to support learning instead of thinking of emotions as impeding learning. What is the role of the student affairs profession in all this?

Our inheritance of the so-called Cartesian split and the intellectual paradigm of Western universities tends to structure most teaching in the positivist tradition of separating observer from observation. We examine data by searching for patterns that can become interpretive principles. For example, we assume the subject/object split in examining data. We learn *about* other cultures rather than experiencing or reflecting on them with a conscious awareness of our own perspective; we study the *impact* of culture on development in contrast to describing the processes by which culture influences development over time. Our metaphors for studying and understanding culture have been noninteractive, reflecting the positivist epistemology. Studies of students and their cultures have historically attempted to establish categories of differentiation among members of different cultures so that people from the dominant culture can understand and respond to students from other cultures appropriately The historical approach has been to treat students from various groups as data sets and then to respond to individuals as if the generic information that has been developed about their identity group were unquestionably accurate in specific situations.

Research has reflected a far more constructivist approach (Abes, Jones, & McEwan, 2007; Diamond & Butterworth, 2008; Literte, 2010). Many students now refuse to deposit themselves into the census boxes or to identify with monoracial cultural centers that have played an important role on campuses since the 1960s (Literte). The people who seem most challenged in understanding the role of cultural lens in interpreting information are members of the dominant White, heterosexual, Christian majority, because their lens remains the dominant interpretive framework in public discourse and is therefore less often subject to powerful challenges. American binary thinking shapes the dominant worldview, and other methods of interpreting information often seem confusing to those who see the world through this lens. A typical question asked of students whose ethnic origins are indeterminate, that is, multiracial, is "What are you?" rather than "Who are you?" This question reflects a need from the questioner to put the new person into a comprehensible category before, or instead of, developing a relationship with that person that acknowledges complexity and change in context.

Anthropologists and other researchers who use ethnographic and phenomenological methods are unlikely to see culture as object and more likely to view it as process. They attempt to see the world through the perspective of culture, looking inward and outward simultaneously while trying to understand how culture shapes perception. They recognize that "there is no point in looking for foundations or using the language of absolute truth. . . . [They] recognize the power of the environment to press for adaptation, the temporality of knowledge and the existence of multiple selves behaving in consonance with the rules of various subcultures" (Noddings, 1990, p. 12). They ask, what's going on here? How are the various elements in this situation interacting? Culture from this perspective is "a process of negotiating power and creating shared meaning through talk" (C. Gailey, personal communication, March 8, 1993). The creation of shared meaning is an element that has appeared in previous definitions. Negotiating power is a new dimension that is applied to analyses of the acculturation of students from nondominant cultures to campus life and to relations among faculty members, students, and administrators. A comprehensive view of the use of multiple lenses and acknowledgment of multiple perspectives in the student affairs literature is Renn and Arnold's (2003) map for reconceptualizing research on student peer culture.

Other disciplines also address the interaction between self and culture in shaping the interpretive lens of the individual. Schweder (1990), a cultural psychologist, describes his field as

> the study of the way cultural traditions and social practices regulate, express, transform and permit the human psyche, resulting less in psychic unity for human kind than in ethnic divergences in mind, self, emotion. . . . [Cultural psychologists] study ways subject and object, self and other, psyche and culture, person and context, figure and group, practitioner and practice live together, require each other and dynamically, dialectically and jointly make each other up. (p. 1)

Cultural psychology assumes that all people live in uncertainty and search for meaning by creating intentional worlds in which "nothing real just is" (p. 4). Intentional worlds are another way of describing lenses. In an intentional world, meaning is constructed by people who are involved in events, observing them, participating in them, and reflecting on them. This approach contrasts with the positivist set of assumptions that things exist independently of human perception and that organizing categories emerge from empirical data with no particular regard for the perspective of the person who is creating categories. Intentional worlds are sociocultural environments that exist "as long as there exists a community of persons whose beliefs, desires, emotions, purposes and other mental representations are directed by it and are thereby influenced by it" (p. 2). Intentional worlds create time-limited cultures, which adds another level to the process of lens construction. From an Afrocentric perspective, this interpenetration is expressed in the aphorism "I am because we are" (Myers, 1993, p. 20). The paradigm of intentional worlds in which "nothing real just is" (Schweder) provides a dramatic contrast to the scientific, positivist paradigm that seeks to discover universal truths that can be expressed in a universal language and remain constant across time and space. Intentionality is based on existential uncertainty and consciousness of human efforts to create meaning in a world of shifting circumstances.

Science is based on the notion of a relatively stable universe in which cause and effect relationships can lead to inference of unchanging principles. Monotheistic religion has also historically focused on applying unchanging principles to the vagaries of human life and attempting to discover the meaning of life through these principles. Metaphorically, the contrast between scientific/monotheistic approaches and constructivist approaches might be compared to stages on the Perry (1968) scale with science and its two-valued logic falling toward the dualistic end of the scheme and intentionality with its multivalued logical/intuitive approach falling toward the commitment-in-relativism end of the continuum. Unfortunately this metaphoric comparison is somewhat misleading. The Perry scheme is hierarchical, with the higher stages conveying a higher level of complexity and sophistication than the lower. To be higher on a hierarchy implies that it is better since hierarchies exist for purposes of tracking progress and determining value. The differences between hierarchical approaches and multifaceted less-hierarchical approaches is more one of style than value. Both are capable of attaining high levels of complexity, albeit based on different approaches to valuing (Baxter Magolda, 1993).

Postmodern psychological theorists also reflect the need for people to develop an awareness of the multiple lenses modern life requires. Gergen (1991), a marriage and family therapist, suggests we should "bid final adieu to the concrete entity of self and then to trace the reconstruction of self as relationship . . . [because] the multiplication of perspectives led to a blurring of boundaries" (p. 140). Gergen believes there is no stable self, or identity, in the absence of relationships, and the only way to create successful relationships is to understand the lens of the other as well as one's own lens in a particular situation that helps to create it.

Positivism and Constructivism

Two branches of philosophy provide the basis for positivist and constructivist approaches to research: ontology, which is the study of the nature of truth, and epistemology, which is the study of the relationship between the knower and the known (Lincoln & Guba, 1985). In the scientific paradigm, truth is unchanging, and the knower observes but does not interact with the known. The basic reality is physical and can be measured, counted and seen, touched, or apprehended in some other physical modality, either by people directly through the senses or by the use of mechanical or chemical instrumentation. In constructivist paradigms, subject and object are always considered interactively, and absolute truth is not a viable construct. Constructivism focuses on relationships and perspectives. The relationships tend to be nonlinear, interactive, and unpredictable, described in terms of probabilities rather than cause and effect. Change is often irreversible because it proceeds in a weblike fashion, not in a straight line. Constructivism tends to look for interactive patterns and trends rather than unidirectional cause and effect events, generally seeking to understand the particular in depth rather than to construct universal explanations for classes of events (Frye, 1990). Realities are considered social constructs that are related to tangible events and objects but whose meanings are constructed by the people who observe, organize, and interpret them (Lincoln & Guba).

Constructivism constitutes an element of the emerging paradigm in student affairs. "The central aspect is a shift from objects to relationships, and story telling supplants classical logic as a way of knowing" (Capra, 1982, p. 78). Since the profession is in the midst of a paradigm shift, and that paradigm fits more effectively with student services work, people who tell stories of particular situations that are pertinent to decisions are often accused of using anecdotal data, which is considered less significant and less reliable than numerical data. The reality seems to be that a combination of stories gathered systematically and analyzed appropriately with numerical, positivist data provides the most reliable method for understanding issues that require responses from student affairs organizations. This emerging combination accounts for the widespread use of focus groups as part of policy-making processes.

Constructivist Perspectives on Science and Education

Constructivism has also become the basis for much of learning theory in K–12 educational systems where students are encouraged to interact with information and create their own applications and meaning for the knowledge they acquire (Caine, Caine, McClintic, & Klimek, 2005). It is used in some areas of higher education, particularly in professional and laboratory-based programs where students must learn skills along with concepts and create applications for particular circumstances. Any discipline in which students are expected to reflect on or discuss their responses to assignments is a site where constructivist teaching and learning can occur.

Constructivism reflects a revision of the scientific paradigm that appeared in physics in the early 20th century in the work of Einstein, Heisenberg, Bohr, Bateson, and Chew (Capra, 1982). Subjectivity and perception became part of the scientific data-gathering process as descriptions of the observer and the observation instruments were integrated into presentations of new information. Heisenberg's uncertainty principle paved the way for increased emphasis on subjectivity and the interaction of cognitive, affective, and interpersonal elements in making meaning and interpreting events. Constructivism opened the door for discussions of the role of consciousness, or mindfulness, in learning and working. Capra (1982) observed that "the basic structures of the material world are determined by the way we look at the world; . . . observed patterns of matter are reflections of patterns of mind" (p. 93). Siegel (2007) has supported Capra's early assertions by discovering that consciousness of thinking, feeling, action, memory, and interpretation all contribute to the integration of knowledge and the capacity to make meaning:

> Vertical integration is the way in which distributed circuits are brought into connection functionally with each other, from head to toe. Here we are focusing on how input from the body is brought up through the spinal cord and bloodstream into the brainstem, limbic areas and cortex to form a vertically integrated circuit. . . . Bringing somatic input into the focus of our attention changes what we can do with the information. Consciousness permits choice and change. (p. 298)

John Dewey's (1916) approach to learning as described in *Democracy and Education* was called *pragmatism* and was a forerunner to constructivism. Seeing that the United States was a dynamic, growing, and multicultural democracy, he emphasized the need for people to learn to work together, create common meaning, and understand multiple perspectives. He emphasized the construction of personal and common meaning using scientific data-gathering methods followed by conversations about implications of new data. He described democracy as "a mode of associated living, of conjoint, communicated experience" (pp. 101–102), which repudiates the principle of external authority, and those involved with democracy search for areas of common concern where citizens can develop responses suited to their best common interests. He observed that "education is a constant reorganizing or reconstructing of experience. It has all the time as an immediate end. . . . the direct transformation of the quality of experience . . . in order to add meaning to the quality of the experience" (pp. 89–90). Dewey suggested that an extremely important task of education in a multicultural democracy was the creation of shared meanings among citizens. This approach is a contrast to later educational philosophies that emphasize the study of presumably static historical American culture in order to integrate oneself into it, adopting its perspective as one's own (Bloom, 1987). Despite the work of Ronald Takaki (2008) and Howard Zinn (Zinn & Arnove, 2004) to present a more accurate description and interpretation of U.S. history, masses of American schoolchildren have learned history the way Bloom described it. The standard approach to learning history is generally not Deweyan, using construction and reconstruction. It involves apprehension, comprehension, and repetition.

It's not *just* an academic difference of opinion.

The contrast between positivist and constructivist approaches to education has powerful implications. When administrators and faculty of humanities departments across the United States started fighting about the content of their courses in the 1970s and 1980s, they were really fighting about the way American culture was to be represented to college students. When students study the historical documents and works of literature, art, and music produced by Americans and Europeans, they are learning about who we think we are as a people (Readings, 1996). If the choice of learning material overwhelmingly reflects the work of "dead White males," as the canon is often referred to, students from an enormous range of other ethnic backgrounds and many women do not see themselves in American culture. When students are expected to learn the contents of these works rather than attempt to discuss and understand the context and consequences, they are learning from a positivist paradigm and may not realize the role perspective plays in the works they study. To the credit of many disciplines, positivist methods are no longer used at the college level in many courses. Unfortunately they continue to be used in the K–12 schools largely because of the political processes involved in buying textbooks and the use of high-stakes achievement tests that demand correct answers to test questions. For student affairs professionals, the consequences of this method of learning history are that students often have great difficulty learning anything from diversity training, an area student affairs is largely responsible for, because they arrive at college thinking all people can be placed into mutually exclusive categories such as race or gender. In addition, student affairs professionals tend to lack the academic expertise to present these issues with the depth and complexity required (McDade, 2005).

One way of understanding the essential conflict between positivism and constructivism is through an observation made by Sancho Panza to Don Quixote in the song lyrics from *Man of La Mancha*: "Whether the stone hits the pitcher or the pitcher hits the stone, it's going to be bad for the pitcher" (www.burbler.com/man-of-la-mancha-soundtrack-a-little-gossip-lyrics.html). Constructivist approaches make point of view explicit and identify biases and assumptions in the perspective of the observer. Constructivist scholarship often discusses power differentials between the observer and the observed (Feigenbaum, 2007; Freire, 1985; Harding, 1991; Seifert, 2007). Positivist approaches make different and contradictory assumptions. Constructivists can afford to protect and tolerate the expression of different perspectives. Even when constructivists are committed to their own perspective and have trouble remaining civil to people who hold different perspectives, philosophically they are committed to the acknowledgment of multiple and different ideas. Constructivists struggle with the problem of developing criteria for evaluating credibility (Patton, 1990), but they do not believe that one perspective should dominate or hold hegemony. Constructivism can tolerate positivism as one perspective, but the reverse is not true.

Positivism assumes that the most valid perspective ought to dominate until a better perspective, which accounts for more data, is articulated.

Therefore a positivist approach cannot logically validate or accept multifaceted constructivist approaches. This is a case of stones and pitchers. Thomas Kuhn (1996) exposed the political influences on changes in scientific, positivist theorizing, but public opinion continues to support the notion that scientific truth exists, and that ultimately it will be discovered. When they are under pressure to make sense out of a disrespectful and frustrating world, constructivists are often accused of dominating or making attempts to impose politically correct views on others. This behavior can be seen as an instance in which emotional needs for expression and a sense of being listened to overwhelm the capacity for intellectual discourse than an aspect of the philosophical approach itself. "When the universe becomes unmanageable, human beings become absolutists" (Bordo, 1987, p. 17).

Both/And

Although positivism and constructivism often have difficulty coexisting, both paradigms have utility in understanding the human experience. In the following section, we examine culture and its function as a paradigm for interpreting human experience from positivist and constructivist perspectives. First, the content of American culture is examined with special attention to the intersection between monotheism, the scientific paradigm, and other elements of Euro-American culture. Second, the processes by which culture changes at the borders is examined, particularly with reference to the scientific culture of American universities and the various constructivist cultures of different student groups and the student affairs profession. Finally we examine the particular point of intersection of these two cultures: the college classroom. The classroom is typically dominated by faculty members trained in the scientific tradition and populated by students who represent many different paradigmatic perspectives but are generally trained to believe in the hegemony of one.

Monotheist Heritage

In 1492 the Western Hemisphere was discovered by Europeans searching for gold and the opportunity to spread Christianity. The United States was settled by people who were searching for individual economic opportunity and religious freedom for their specific groups. Our Constitution forbids establishing a state-endorsed religion. Nevertheless, Christianity is the privileged faith in the United States, and Judaism is tolerated because it arrived at the beginning of European settlement. The founders of the United States did not want to create religious freedom in the modern sense. They wanted freedom to practice their approach to Christianity without interference from others. They did not tolerate atheists. They killed people, mostly women, who practiced the ancient earth religions and considered Native people heathens. They considered Christianity the one true faith. The Christian articulation of God, while espousing kindness and compassion, also supported killing enemies and destroying the holy places of competing faith groups (Armstrong, 1993). Islam did not appear in the early history of North America. Despite its status as one of the three Abramic faiths (Armstrong), Islam has never held equal status to Judaism or Christianity in the United States and has suffered from great abuse and discrimination since the beginning of the terrorist jihads conducted in the name of that faith.

Scientism

Americans tend to believe in science and the knowledge it generates as the ultimate credible source of truth. This belief has led American culture toward a perspective called *scientism* (Wilber, 2001), a belief that countable data constitute the most reliable reality, and that reality generated from personal analysis, insight, or historical revelation is less reliable. Wilber asserted there are at least three valid ways of knowing, or sets of criteria for reliability: the eye of the flesh (material reality), the eye of the mind (reality generated from analytical though), and the eye of contemplation (theological and intuitive reality). The perspective of scientism has frequently been discounted, even by scientists, and is a reflection of the positivism/constructivism conflict. As a people we tend to believe that seeing (or touching, feeling, measuring, or counting) should be believing or at least trusting the evidence of our senses. We hold this belief so strongly that it impinges on beliefs espoused by religion and undermines our faith in our own intellect and intuition. The term *scientism* was coined to describe our faith in the scientific, materialist perspective as the only source of truth and the rejection of other sources of insight and information. Many atheistic Americans tend to hold this belief as dogmatically as some hold religious beliefs.

In the United States logical reasoning has more credibility than intuition or experiential ways of knowing, such as exploring dreams for deeper meanings or going on a vision quest to help make a decision or set a life direction.

Arguments that are supported by data are considered more powerful than arguments supported by religious beliefs or value statements. Empirical evidence, be it financial, behavioral, political, or geographical, typically has more credibility than omens, inspirations, or contacts from disembodied spirits. Large amounts of data that support existing theories, belief systems, or values have the most credibility of all, even though these databases can be manipulated to support perspectives that are unacknowledged. Sociologists, economists, natural scientists, and other interpreters of mass amounts of data are listened to endlessly. They provide us with culturally acceptable truths in culturally acceptable forms. Unless, of course, we don't want to believe them for unacknowledged reasons. The debate over climate change is one example of that process. The data supporting evidence of large shifts in climate abound, but somehow oil companies and other groups that benefit from our carbon-burning economic system don't agree with the conclusions this evidence seems to support.

Materialistic Assumptions

Materialism has several meanings. The first refers to the hegemony of empirical data. The second refers to an emphasis on acquisition of material goods and evaluating a person's worth by the amount of material possessions she or he accumulates (e.g., the bumper sticker slogan, "The boy who dies with the most toys wins"). In the United States, more is usually better, and the garbage dumps continue to overflow. Historically, the emphasis on materialism is connected to scientific traditions and the early history of mercantilism in the New World. The Puritans believed idleness was sinful and wealth was a sign of God's grace. A final element of materialism is the national preoccupation with physical appearance, a single standard of beauty, and the notion that anything that appears wrong with a person should be either fixed or covered up. Materialism does not necessarily imply decadence, but it does become dangerous when it is emphasized to the exclusion of other aspects of the culture. When Donald Trump becomes a national icon, perhaps he is serving as the canary in the mine.

Assimilationist Ideology

Assimilationist ideology has been a central part of our national thinking since we adopted *E pluribus unum* as our national motto. Our approach to bringing unity from the diversity of the many peoples who arrived in North

America has been to deculture all groups who were not members of the original founding groups from England, Scotland, and other parts of Europe. As soon as Africans began to be imported as slaves, race became a defining element in American identity. Race increased in importance throughout the 17th century for economic and political reasons. It was embedded in the Constitution when slaves were defined as property and counted as three fifths of a person for census purposes. Difference has always mattered in the United States—visible differences as described by skin color and cultural differences as described by variations in emotional expressiveness, time orientation, family construction, work ethic, and emphasis on the relative value of materialism and spirituality (Okun, Fried, & Okun, 1999). Immigrants whose living patterns most closely approximated those of the English blended in the most easily. In succeeding generations, the other groups often attempted to eliminate their differences from the dominant group through name changes, emphasis on family privacy, religious changes, and more recently, plastic surgery.

Liberal Democracy and Individual Rights

Liberalism has often been misunderstood and misrepresented in political discourse. The philosophical foundation of the United States is based on two assumptions that constitute liberalism: The welfare of the individual is of paramount importance and, "The relationships between individuals in a community are irreducibly moral relationships" (Sabine, 1961, p. 745). Conceptually there is no conflict between attending to the needs of an individual and maintaining a community because human beings are social beings and require community. The basis of morality is considered to be the capacity for empathy because empathy permits one person to "feel [the] subjective experiences" (Siegel, 2007, p. 355) of another person and thus treat that person as we would want to be treated. "The result would be greater ability to stay open with others, even in the face of their distress" (p. 355). The capacity to empathize and develop trusting, moral relationships is hardwired into the brain.

Operationally, one major role of government is to balance the needs of any particular individual or group with the needs of the larger community to maintain both sides. Lately, political discourse has pitted the needs of the individual, or classes of individuals, against the government as a representation of the national group or national welfare. This is a misrepresentation of the original meaning of *liberal*. Liberalism is about maximizing individual freedom in a context that includes everyone else's freedom and opportunity. The aphorism "Your freedom to swing your arm ends where my nose begins" is an illustration of this principle. The tension is continuous and therefore leads to a corollary: the profound reliance of liberal democracies on the value of free speech and the marketplace of ideas as a means of seeking solutions to problems. Efforts to suppress debate, despite the discomfort debate may bring, are efforts to suppress a basic operating principle of liberal democracy. These democracies employ constituent assemblies and elected officials who are expected to conduct business in public and be responsible to voters.

Individual interests have traditionally been considered the most important interests in liberal democracies. A major source of morality in these democracies is the assumption that people should be treated as ends in themselves and not be considered as means to ends. "A community exists because the people in it do more or less recognize each other as ends or sources of value and therefore as beings having rights which a moral claim on the obligations that these rights impose" (Sabine, 1961, p. 744). The conversation about rights and obligations must be continuous as society changes, wealth flows from one economic site to another, and different groups achieve or lose political power. Since liberalism arose as part of the European Enlightenment, it also asserts that individuals act *rationally*, in their *enlightened self-interest*. This assumption leads to the emphasis in democratic societies on education, free access to information, and freedom of speech. This belief in enlightened self-interest as the major motivator underlies the theory of free market capitalism and the "science" of economics. Fundamental to this position is that if economic humans operate in their enlightened self-interest, economic markets will prosper. All of these assumptions have been challenged repeatedly in the recurring cycle of boom and bust characteristic of capitalistic economies.

Liberalism differentiates between society and government. Society is pluralistic, filled with many groups that command allegiance from their members and have shared interests that conflict with the interests of other groups. Society is disorganized and not structured according to any comprehensive principles. Government is much more limited. It is organized for the purpose of keeping options open for individuals. De Tocqueville (1835/1956) was describing American society rather than American government when he called individualism an erroneous judgment that originated from the deficiencies of the mind. Individualism, as an absolute belief system, causes people to separate themselves from the community and operate as if community responsibilities including everything from trash removal, nutrition for children, education, and maintaining community infrastructure were all concerns best left to individuals. Taking your own trash to the dump, a feasible choice in rural communities, simply does not work in urban situations. Paving the road in front of your own house rarely works anywhere. De Tocqueville (1835/1956) observed that Americans had a tendency to focus on individualism as the pursuit of self-interest in a manner that sapped the virtues of public life and ultimately degenerated into selfishness. This tendency has ebbed and flowed in our history (Levine, 1980) and has been in a period of ascendency since the 1970s. "American cultural traditions define personality, achievement and the purpose of human life in ways that leave the individual in glorious but terrifying isolation" (Bellah et al., 1985, p. 6) The economic crisis of 2008 seems to have exerted a major push on the public mind, shifting the pendulum in the opposite direction. As of this writing it seems too soon to be sure.

American belief in the primacy of the individual amplifies the positivist belief in facts without context and the objectivist belief in the observer's separation from events observed. "This ideal of freedom has historically given Americans a respect for individuals. . . . sometimes even made them tolerant of differences. . . . [but it] leaves Americans with a stubborn fear of acknowledging structures of power and interdependence" (Bellah et al., 1985, p. 25). It also leaves Americans with a naïveté about the effects of culture in shaping perceptions, values, and behavior. Americans tend to believe that all choices are individual choices, made with little awareness of history, context, or culture. This tendency seems to be a more accurate description of White Americans than any other group because they may remain unaware of the influences identified.

The American legal system has codified this dimension of the cultural paradigm. Legal conflicts are couched in the language of conflicting rights and resolved by establishing one set of rights over another. Legal discourse is governed by rules of logic and evidence. Issues of hate speech and First Amendment rights of free speech are particularly difficult to resolve in this format because context and impact must be reduced to the language of individual rights. Although critical legal scholars have attempted to place the law in a broader social, political, and historical context, their work has gone largely unnoticed by the American public and remains highly controversial (Matsuda, Lawrence, Delgado, & Crenshaw, 1993). Efforts to regulate hate speech on campus as a means of decreasing intergroup conflict have been largely unsuccessful because of the focus on conflicting rights and the primacy of the individual's right to free speech.

In short, our cultural focus on individualism makes the very notion of group-oriented identity difficult for White Americans to comprehend. This undermines our ability to see ourselves as members of communities without perceiving our membership as a threat to our freedom. This dynamic operates differently in communities where one or more significant aspect of identity influences perspective, including communities of color, immigrant communities, communities of people with disabilities, and others. Members of these groups have often experienced the strength that derives from acting together and learn to balance the needs of the group with their own needs. The belief in individualism as a rigid construct impedes our ability to see each other as complex cultural beings or to recognize that our inevitable conflicts often have origins that are much broader than simple interpersonal dislikes or conflicts of interest. The legal structure we use to maintain order reinforces individualism and provides very little support for balanced notions of individual and group responsibility. The historical emphasis on personal mobility and independence, the scientific training that de-emphasizes context, the materialistic focus that emphasizes appearance and ignores nonmaterial information all interact to produce individuals who see the world through a lens called *I*, shaped by personal experience and limited to the perspective developed in a single lifetime.

Principles of the American Cultural Paradigm

- Monotheism, scientism, and assimilationism have at least one element in common. They all support the notion that *there is always a best answer or explanation*, and that it is singular rather than complex. Monotheism prescribes belief and behavior. Scientism looks for unifying principles, emphasizing patterns, and throwing out anomalies. Assimilationism focuses on integrating members of nondominant groups into the dominant group, not on celebrating differences.
- American two-valued logic, derived from monotheism and scientism, supports hierarchical thinking. In hierarchies, there is always a best

way. Therefore we have trouble understanding that if one experience or trait is good, another can be equally good even if different. For example, if black is good, white is bad; if logic is good, feelings must be less good; if rich is good, poor must be terrible.

- Materialism has trained Americans to trust physical evidence and doubt all other evidence. This perspective leads to such commonplace comments as, "You can't argue with the bottom line" or "Let the facts speak for themselves." This makes challenging the process to determine the facts or the bottom line difficult to impossible.

- Individualism and a powerful emphasis on rights as opposed to responsibilities has left Americans with a strong mistrust of any force that suggests that some aspect of individual freedom or gain should be sacrificed for the common good or for the benefit of the less fortunate except in times of natural crisis such as floods, fires, or earthquakes.

- Individualism, in combination with materialism, implies that a person should be able to do whatever he or she wishes to the environment, physical or human, because that person is separate from and uninfluenced by the environment. Mutual shaping has not been assumed until recently, when the drastic effects of human behavior on the global environment have become quite apparent.

- Americans tend to believe, for the most part, that reality is out there to be discovered, not in here, organized if not created, in the mind of the observer. Because of the factors discussed in this chapter, many Americans tend to think they are observing and reacting to a world that exists beyond themselves, whose meaning they have no part in constructing and that for the most part they are powerless to change.

This paradigm has enormous implications for the ability of the United States to create a truly diverse society, one that accepts the existence of multiple perspectives without needing to decide which one is true. It also has implications for the ways we think about and engage in teaching and learning and the ways student affairs professionals relate to other members of campus communities.

5

TELESCOPES AND KALEIDOSCOPES
Lenses That Focus Our Vision

I n the preceding chapters, three words were used almost interchangeably: paradigm, culture, and lens. The words have very different meanings but can be considered as three ways of describing the process people use to make sense of information and organize, interpret, and use it.

Paradigm

A paradigm is a frame of reference, a set of assumptions for interpreting the masses of data we apprehend (Kolb, 1984). Paradigms can be described as "a distillation of what we think about the world (but cannot prove)" (Lincoln & Guba, 1985, p. 15) or as systems of ideas along with methods of learning and understanding. The notion of paradigm and paradigm shift has been widely discussed in the physical sciences (Kuhn, 1996; Wheatley, 1999), the social and behavioral sciences (Caple, 1991; Lincoln & Guba), and business (Wheatley).

Kuhn (1996) used the term *paradigm* to indicate the means that define legitimate problems in a particular field of study. For example, the scientific paradigm defines problems as those that involve data and phenomena that can be observed, measured, and replicated under controlled circumstances. A scientific problem might involve studying the behavior of a virus in a particular environment such as the human bloodstream. A legitimate problem in the social sciences would involve studying the behavior of voters in particular electoral regions or with regard to specific political issues. In student affairs, the study of factors affecting student attrition and persistence is a legitimate problem that is studied continuously. The second way Kuhn uses *paradigm* is to describe legitimate research methods used to generate reliable information about those problems. In studying a virus, standard laboratory procedures are used, and only data gathered using those procedures are considered reliable. In studying the HIV virus, for example, researchers use various inquiry methods to understand the biochemical structures of the virus and its means of replication, and experiment with various methods of disrupting replication. No scientific HIV researcher would take a vial of HIV-infected blood to the top of a mountain, tie it from a cord around her or his neck, and fast and mediate on the mountaintop for 40 days as a means of finding a cure. A mystically oriented scientist might do something comparable, such as going on a retreat to think about the problem, but the results of the research would never be reported in those terms because the terms don't fit the accepted paradigm for scientific research. The scientist would return to the lab and test the insights using standard scientific methods. If the research confirmed the mystical insights, the results would be reported as scientific results not revelations.

The dominant paradigm in a discipline tells practitioners and researchers what to think about and how to investigate. In student affairs the dominant paradigm focuses on inquiry about student life outside the classroom in such areas as identity formation (Abes, Jones, & McEwan, 2007) in its increasingly complex forms, intra- and interpersonal competence, practical competence, persistence and academic achievement, humanitarianism, and civic engagement. The learning outcomes listed in *Learning Reconsidered* (Keeling, 2004) also include cognitive complexity and knowledge acquisition and integration, but the majority of student affairs research has been conducted in the first group of domains, all of which occur predominantly outside the classroom. The underlying divisions between academic learning, experiential learning, and personal reflection remain firmly in place. Methods for investigation within this paradigm tend to be derived from the same types of scientific empirical methods used widely in the other behavioral sciences. Quantitative and qualitative methods of investigation are used. The methodology of the qualitative work has shifted significantly to reveal the researcher's perspectives and biases so that presumptive objectivity is no longer assumed to be the highest level of interpretation or the sole arbiter of credible knowledge (Evans, Forney, Guido, Patton, & Renn, 2010). Quantitative research retains the assumption that viewpoint is irrelevant and that truth is invariant even when it is incomplete. A number of challenges to the dominant paradigm have been published, including *Learning Partnerships: Theory and Models of Practice to Educate for Self-Authorship,* (Baxter Magolda & King, 2004), *Learning Reconsidered* (Keeling, 2004), and this work. In these documents the academic/student affairs distinction is revealed as ineffective for understanding the learning processes, and methods of integrated teaching/learning are proposed. Baxter Magolda and King have three core assumptions about learning: "Knowledge is complex and socially constructed; identity plays a central role in crafting knowledge claims and knowledge is mutually constructed via the sharing of expertise and authority" (p. xix). In making this assertion, Baxter Magolda and King challenge the paradigm that has shaped our understanding of learning since Descartes first exclaimed "I think, therefore I am." This focus on all aspects of a student's life and learning actually constitutes a reemergence of an earlier paradigm presented in the 1937 *Student Personnel Point of View* (Saddlemire & Rentz, 1986) and explained in greater detail in *A Student Personnel Program for Higher Education* (Lloyd-Jones & Smith, 1938).

Culture

The academic/student affairs split in higher education reflects the Cartesian mind/body split that has dominated higher education since the formation of modern universities and has pervaded Western culture since the 17th century. Culture can be considered one type of paradigm members of a particular culture use to experience and interpret their world. Cultural paradigms are a product of national/ethnic history, religious belief systems, family values, and an almost infinite number of other elements. For purposes of this discussion, culture signifies an understanding that people have of their universe that guides their interpretation of events as well as their expectations and actions in that universe (Ogbu, 1990). Culture in this sense emerges in any group that shares a set of common experiences. For example, gay men who are now in their 50s and older experienced the AIDS epidemic as a certain death sentence. With the development of antiviral drugs to treat HIV, AIDS has been transmuted into a chronic illness that can generally be managed for a long time. These two different experiences of being gay and associated behavioral norms for relationships have created two drastically different generations of men living with HIV. Women who were raised in a world in which their anticipated future included marriage, child rearing, and potential employment in only three or four areas (nursing, teaching, secretarial, hairdressing) have had a very different life experience than women who grew up in the age of Title IX of the Education Amendments of 1972, equal opportunity, and high expectations for individual achievement. In each case, members of a group see the world differently, interpret events differently, and have different expectations of the ways the world will treat them.

Lens

Individuals see and interpret the world through a combination of paradigms that involve philosophical and personal elements, overlap, occasionally conflict, and interact within a very broad frame of reference. In the United States the frame of reference, or national paradigm, is constructed from the elements described in Chapter 4. Lens is a metaphor for the particular paradigm an individual uses to view and interpret a situation at a particular time in a particular context. Lenses can be understood as the interpretive framework in which individual experience and cultural heritage combine. Ho (1995) has suggested the concept of internalized culture as a way to describe the processes that create lenses: "Internalized culture may be defined as the cultural influences operating within the individual that shape (not determine) personality formation and various aspects of psychological functioning" (p. 5). Lenses can be changed as long as people know they are using them. Lenses exist, metaphorically, in arrangements that change the same way the optometrist changes lenses in the diagnostic equipment during an eye examination. The physician asks the patient to look through different lenses and compare them to decide which one is clearer, which one feels more comfortable, and which combination allows the patient to see the best. Different elements of a cultural paradigm become salient depending on the circumstances a person is dealing with at a particular time. It is often tempting to use familiar lenses that distort rather than to endure the disorientation or discomfort of using more accurate lenses in a new situation.

Problems are likely to arise when an individual doesn't realize he or she is using a lens to perceive and interpret a situation. People who interpret the world through dualistic or early multiplistic perspectives do not value different viewpoints or may not realize that different viewpoints exist (Perry, 1968). Every question is presumed to have one answer, and when there is more than one possible answer, the person generally assumes that someone who should know the answer is confused. People who see the world dualistically do not know lenses exist. They often disparage the value of other people's ideas, other ways of doing things and interpreting events, get into conflicts, and cause difficulty in problem solving. Unfortunately, this type of discourse seems to have dominated political conversations during the U.S. 2010 electoral campaigns, and the resulting anger and misunderstanding is altogether too visible.

Lenses function unconsciously unless they are challenged, or a contrasting, credible view appears. Different perspectives are most likely to be acknowledged in low-threat, low-risk environments and rejected in high-threat situations. Among people who share a common unexamined viewpoint, the validity of their lens is taken for granted. Information interpreted through these lenses is believed to be true because the interpreter is often unaware of the interpretive process. The different interpretations of the O. J. Simpson verdict in his murder trial illustrates this point. Black groups and White groups interpreted the same data in almost mutually exclusive ways, and both felt betrayed by the failure of the other group to acknowledge their perspective. On a broader scale, we often hear commentary about terrorists who are exploding bombs among civilians in war-ravaged areas where foreign soldiers are present. Are these people terrorists or freedom fighters? The answer to that question depends on whether the observer is a citizen of the country where the war is happening or a noncitizen victim of the hostilities.

Paradigm Creation

Lenses as Personal Constructs

Paradigms help people impose mental road maps on complex, confusing, or novel situations. Kelly's (1955) theory of personal constructs offers a way of describing the process people use to develop personal lenses. Kelly describes the way people perceive and interpret events as the creation of a series of binary constructs such as good/bad, easy/hard, big/little. These constructs serve as hypotheses to explain what is happening, help the person compare this situation to previous similar situations, predict what is likely to happen next, and decide how to respond. For example, when a person comes to a street corner and sees a traffic light, she or he views the situation as follows:

> Red/green . . . choose green; go/stop . . . choose go; safe/dangerous . . . choose safe; on this corner cars usually obey the light/don't obey the light . . . choose obey; *Action* . . . the person crosses the street.

When perceiving another person walking toward him or her, the first person will also generate a series of binary constructions that compare this person to others and that suggest subsequent actions.

Research on decision making (Caine & Caine, 2006) differentiates between decision making in deterministic versus ambiguous situations. When a person needs to make a decision in a deterministic situation such as filling out forms with mutually exclusive categories or answering questions that have one right answer, the process seems to follow Kelly's (1955) description. However, in situations that are ambiguous and complex, the decision maker uses actor-centered decision making (ACADM; Goldberg, 2001), which also involves weighing priorities and taking context into account. Skill in ACADM also involves managing emotions, taking time into account, and generally accessing the parts of the brain that communicate between thinking and feeling processes. Most real-life situations and decisions involve the use of the ACADM processes, which are also the situations in which student affairs professionals help students learn.

When perceiving another person walking toward him or her, a person may generate a series of binary constructs or engage in the ACADM process. If using a simple binary approach, the following is likely to occur:

> Familiar/strange . . . choose familiar; pleasant/unpleasant . . . choose pleasant; close friend/acquaintance . . . choose acquaintance. *Action* . . . Say hi, wave, or smile, and keep walking.

If the approaching individual is perceived as significantly different, emotions are more likely to come into awareness and influence the decision about responding. Perhaps person one is a five-foot six-inch tall White female who lived with her parents in an all-White suburb and never knew a person whose skin is darker or who is larger than she is and wears a lot of large jewelry. She may have seen such people on television and associates them with criminal behavior. When person two who fits this description approaches her, she has a more complicated challenge in deciding how to respond. She has to apprehend and interpret what the person looks like, respond to her own emotional reaction, possibly remember what people who look like that person are associated with in her memory, and she is probably unaware of most of the reactions she is experiencing except for fear. If the White woman has not learned how to manage her emotions in this kind of situation, or can't calm down quickly enough to simply keep walking, she is likely to make a decision to diminish her own proximity to this stranger. Thus, from a neurological perspective her fears have been reinforced by her decision, and she has not learned anything about how to respond to a novel situation. This lack of skill is the basis of much stereotyping. If one responds to a new and slightly frightening situation by reinforcing habitual behavior, old patterns become stronger. If one consciously chooses a new response to the situation, old patterns are diminished. The presence of these kinds of situations on campus can lead to a great deal of learning about adapting to novel situations and diminishing fear of difference if students learn the necessary self-observation and behavioral change skills.

Neurological reactions to events that demand decisions are shaped by ingrained brain states (Siegel, 2007). These sets of neural correlations make up the organizational system and processes the brain uses to wire together memory, interpretation, and action. Siegel asserts that embedded beliefs that are created very early in our lives, "enslave" (p. 137) us to preconceived ideas and judgments. According to Siegel's research the only way to dismantle these brain states is to experience them in real situations, reflect on personal reactions, question assumptions, and attend to the reality of the experience as it actually occurred. Siegel's description of dismantling neural architecture parallels Kolb's (1984) description of experiential learning and points directly to the process used by individuals to develop their cultural lenses. Siegel clearly believes that preconceived ideas embedded in our neural architecture can be dismantled by a combination of experiential and cognitive learning processes that allow us to reframe our interpretation of and reaction to differences. This integrated learning process is fundamental to the educational role of student affairs. Siegel has clarified the reasons simply learning new information about threatening phenomena does not change our behavior. It is an easy journey from this insight to understanding why a lot of diversity training is not effective. People are not prone to change their minds or their belief systems when they are afraid, and they are not likely to get beyond their fear if they are unaware of their belief system. Siegel's research, along with the work of Zull (2002) in *The Art of Changing the Brain* and Hanson (2009), also provide the keys to understanding transformative learning and their biological underpinnings.

Culture as a Frame for Personal Lenses

Ogbu (1990) defined culture as a system of beliefs that tells us who we are and what we should expect from the world. Siegel (2007) has described the process we use to learn everything that has emotional significance for us, including our sense of culture. Our culturally framed lenses serve as epistemological and ontological guides to help us decide what is real and understand how reality can be known. In the day-to-day course of life, most people are unaware of their cultural and personal lenses, which appear as simply common sense or the way things are. In novel situations we create new lenses or personal paradigms based, to the extent possible, on preexisting neural architecture. Unless we are in the midst of a personal crisis, we simply rearrange the deck chairs on the Titanic. Adolescent girls, for example, face the challenge of maintaining their friendships in the presence of interpersonal or moral conflicts that seem to increase in frequency as they mature and their lives become more complex. They develop a relationship paradigm that permits them to reconcile conflict and maintain friendship through extensive discussion of their values, their concern for each other, and the models of balance and compromise each girl developed as she grew up in her own family (Gilligan, Lyons, & Hanmer, 1990). In Muslim cultures, individuals often rely on precepts from the Koran in deciding how to make sense out of events, how to treat other people, how to dress, and what to eat. Trying to understand and carry out the will of Allah becomes paramount. In many Asian cultures the Tao exerts a strong influence. People are likely to be patient because they expect events to follow a course that ought not to be interfered with. Ultimately, people who adopt the Tao as a paradigm believe that balance restores itself. Whatever actions are taken should follow the natural flow of events, not contradict it. A Taoist would react differently to a corrupt politician than would a member of any political party in the United States. In American jargon the Taoist would see the politician as inevitably failing because corruption contains the seeds of its own destruction. The

American would be more likely to throw the scoundrel out in the next election. An American Taoist might observe that what goes around, comes around.

The ultimate paradigm might be considered the one that provides the broadest possible explanation for the very large amount of information people have to respond to in their lives. Historically, religion and philosophy have provided very general paradigms to help people make sense of their lives. In some times and places, monotheistic religions have served as governing paradigms. In other times and places, nontheistic philosophical approaches have served the same ends. In the 21st-century Western world, the dominant paradigm is largely based on the principles of empirical science as they were developed during the Renaissance and Enlightenment by scientists such as Newton, Copernicus, Bacon, Galileo, and their intellectual heirs. These principles govern our ideas about reliable knowledge and inquiry methods. They contain underlying assumptions about order, predictability, cause and effect relationships, objectivity and single perspective explanations, the primacy of logic, and the necessity of empirical evidence to substantiate beliefs. This paradigm achieved its highest level of utility and accuracy in the field of Newtonian physics (Capra, 1982). To test the significance of this paradigm in your own thinking, try to imagine how you would make sense of a world in which any of the elements described in the following section were not considered true or accurate.

The Scientific Paradigm

The Newtonian paradigm dominated physical and social science research throughout the late 19th and most of the 20th century. With its emphasis on prediction and control, it has been responsible for expanding our understanding of the material world, but this expansion has come at a cost. The paradigm has established borders to our understanding and placed lenses on our perception that mask significant elements of the human experience, particularly those that arise from spirituality, interpersonal relationships, intuition, and personal experience. This is the belief system Wilber (2001) called *scientism*. This paradigm dominates the cultures of the North Atlantic: Europe, the United States, and Canada (West, 1993b). Paradigms that emphasize understanding and unity are rooted in African, Asian, and indigenous worldviews. These paradigms tend to emphasize self-knowledge as the root of all knowledge and the connectedness of perception, knowledge, relationships, and wisdom (American Psychological Association, 2005). An examination of the Afrocentric paradigm highlights the borders of the scientific, Eurocentric paradigm. Thus the borders of the scientific paradigm become clear as assumptions, not presentations of things as they are.

The scientific paradigm has roots in various aspects of Western philosophy whose names, such as materialism, positivism, objectivism, have been used in confusing and interchangeable fashion. The following questions are designed to personalize those elements of the reader's worldview that are grounded in the scientific paradigm.

1. The paradigm assumes that concepts or empirical categories can be defined by direct reference to "objects in concrete" (Lincoln & Guba, 1985, p. 20) or things that exist materially in the physical world. Reality is considered synonymous with physical reality, and external reality has more validity than subjective experience. What is real exists in the physical world and can be observed, measured, and counted.

   Questions: What kinds of realities can you describe that are nonmaterial or nonphysical? Do they seem as real to you as tables and chairs? Your answer shows you how objectivism shapes your perspective.

2. The paradigm assumes the independence and separation of the observer from the observed. Events occur whether or not anybody is there to observe them. Point of view, perspective, or frame of reference are not taken into account when reporting observations. Observers are considered interchangeable because the world exists "out there," and the observer, human, mechanical, or electronic, merely records what is. Data exist independently of theory or interpretation in what is also called a "correspondence theory of truth" (Lincoln & Guba, 1985, p. 24). Truth is assumed to correspond to accurate descriptions of data. Categories of analysis are discovered by the researcher, not seen as human constructs data are organized around to create meaning. Challenges to this worldview are based on the notion that reality is more complex than a single perspective and that all observation is interpretation. There is simply no way of experiencing external reality except through some limited form of perception that inevitably shapes interpretation.

Questions: If two people were standing in the forest and a tree fell, would they both hear the same sounds? If a Hindu and a Christian were walking in the woods and came upon a swarm of bees, would they both have the same experience or react the same way? If an African American and a Euro-American were sitting in the same classroom and the professor said, "Let's call a spade a spade," would the sentence mean the same thing to both Americans? Does the phrase "Get real" signify to you that you are thinking about the impossible or the unacceptable and that somebody who is more realistic is trying to get you back into the acceptable paradigm?

3. The paradigm is grounded in two-valued logic in which all data are evaluated according to whether they fit into a theoretical interpretation. The goal of two-valued logic is to develop categories of analysis that account for the largest amount of data and minimize the range of data that cannot be understood. Research based on eliminating the null hypothesis is organized in this fashion. Data frequently fit into more than two categories. Some fit the theory and are included. For example, students who are struggling with choice of vocation or finding ways to develop intimate relationships fit into Chickering's (Chickering & Reisser, 1993) theory of identity formation. Some data challenge the theory and are excluded. For example, students whose main concern is finding enough time to spend with their children while working and going to school do not seem to fit into any of the original categories related to identity formation and are therefore excluded from the theory. Finally, some data cannot be accounted for by the theory and are considered ambiguous or anomalous and are not discussed. For example, African American students may be creating an identity that includes developing emotional control but also emphasizes spiritual development and relationships with family more strongly than traditional-age Euro-American students. African Americans display some characteristics in common with students described by the original theory and some concerns that are not accounted for. As theories evolve, previously unexplained phenomena are included and explained so that theory can keep pace with increasing complexity. Current research on identity formation (Abes, Jones, & McEwan, 2007) is far more complex than Chickering's

early work and accounts for identity development processes in a much broader range of students. In constructing theory, errors always occur. The goal is to develop categories that keep the undecided middle ground as small as possible (Ziman, 1978). In the positivist, objectivist approach to category construction issues of value and power are not discussed. Scientists' values are assumed not to play a role in the process. Challenges to this point of view have been raised by feminists in particular.

Questions: What do you do when you have data you can't explain? Do you try to create an explanation, expand your paradigm, ignore or discount it, or put it on hold until an explanation presents itself? How do you explain the presence of very bright students on campus who can't get grades above a C no matter how hard they try? Does intelligence level help us understand why women are so heavily outnumbered in engineering or men in nursing but not in physicians assistant programs? Why do supposedly nice guys occasionally rape women or sometimes other men? What do you do when your theories, lenses, or personal constructs do not satisfactorily explain what's going on in your world?

4. The paradigm has a number of other scientific characteristics. It uses deductive thinking based on hypotheses that are developed logically and tested empirically (Patton, 1990). It assumes a uniformity of nature across time and space and does not acknowledge the effect of context. It assumes that the larger the data set, the more generally true and universally accurate the analyses may be. It also assumes that a universal scientific language can be developed to describe physical reality so that all scientists will be able to understand descriptions in a similar fashion (Lincoln & Guba, 1985). It assumes cause and effect relationships that are incremental, mechanical, and traceable backward in time (Caple, 1987). It assumes that culture has little to do with perception and nothing to do with science. It asserts that "all aspects of complex phenomena can be understood by reducing them to their constituent parts" (Capra, 1982, p. 59).

Questions: What does it mean to tell the truth as a witness in an auto accident case? Does the corner where the witness was standing shape the witness's account of what really happened?

The Limits of the Scientific Paradigm

The scientific paradigm, which has tremendous utility in helping people understand, predict, and control their environments, has serious limitations when used to develop a system of morality and values for human societies or as the only means to understand and interpret human behavior. When this paradigm governs research in the social sciences, humans are treated as data sets that are not significantly different from other physical phenomena whose behavior is governed by universal impersonal laws. For example, those in sociology study humans in the aggregate and attempt to discover universal truths about the behavior of humans in groups. The social and behavioral sciences tend to reify or make things out of events and relationships, giving them the appearance of independent, decontextualized existence, separate from human interpretation. This approach reflects the empirical or material-istic assumptions of the scientific paradigm. It seriously distorts research data that fall into the middle category of no explanation or anomaly. This tends to include the data seen through personal lenses and cultural paradigms, par-ticularly those related to faith, intuition, personal loyalty, and other nonma-terial phenomena. These types of beliefs exert powerful influences on human behavior but are extremely difficult to quantify. In these situations, the limits of the scientific paradigm, the boundaries of its utility, are highlighted and made visible. It presents information with misleading certainty and often ignores information because it does not fit into scientific categories. In other words, this lens does not show us everything it purports to show. It is better at showing us outcomes or effects of large trends on massive numbers of people than it is on showing us particular and individual processes by which people change or develop insight and make meaning in their lives (Parks, 2000). Data collected and presented as variables are data reduced and taken out of context. The resulting picture is incomplete, failing to present the whole picture of the complex human experience.

This paradigm is so pervasive that it does not appear in day-to-day life as a set of assumptions about the world. It appears as the way things are, reflecting an attitude about reality, objectivity, and reasonableness. As a culture we believe in the trustworthiness of facts, pieces of noncontextual information. We tend to trust data presented in statistical form more than any other type of data. We ask for the bottom line as measured numeri-cally. We are reluctant to rely on anecdotal evidence because we are not sure how valid it is, that is, how large a percentage of the total data universe it represents. People who address problems by relying on gut instincts are generally considered less reliable than people who make decisions on the basis of facts. The entire assessment and accountability movement in higher education represents this excessive reliance on quantifiable data. Evidence is now emerging that assessment that examines transformative learning is now integrating qualitative assessment methodologies into the overall process of assessing learning, but quantitative methodologies seem to remain dominant at this time (Wehlberg, 2008). Increasing financial stress on institutions will probably support increasing reliance on quantitative methods and the measure of cost-effectiveness of programs without clearly articulating the value these programs add for students or institutions in qualitative terminology.

Seeing the world through the assumptions of the scientific paradigm, Americans often seem to rely on two-valued logic illustrated by such mottos as "America, love it or leave it," and "If guns are outlawed, only outlaws will have guns." Talk shows that present complex problems like domestic violence, sexual behavior, gun control, and hate speech flourish on daytime television by pitting one oversimplified point of view against another. Pseudolegal shows such as *Judge Judy* take this process to the extreme because somebody always wins and there is always a loser, and the process rarely takes more than an hour to complete. Campus hate speech regulations adopt an either/or approach that pits the rights of one person or group against another rather than attempting to judge the effect or intention of the speech in the context it occurred, and encourage the parties involved to develop a more complex understanding of their differences. Despite the existence of a number of schemes of cognitive and moral development that describe the ability to manage complex and interacting ideas as the hallmark of sophistication and wisdom (Baxter Magolda, 1993; King & Kitchener, 1994; Perry, 1968), a desire for correct answers seems to dominate national discourse. The No Child Left Behind high-stakes testing movement simply exacerbates this national tendency. Children who go to school under this policy have no choice but to believe that every question has a right answer and that it is their responsibility to be able to express those answers on tests.

Our national belief that reality exists "out there" and that change occurs in a simple cause and effect process also reflects the domination of the scientific paradigm in the American cultural perspective. Marginal or nondominant groups that view events differently are often ignored because their version of reality strains the paradigm. For example, from the materialist perspective, military spending is more important than spending on the humanities. Artists have appeared before Congress to request that appropriations for the arts and humanities be increased. The artists described how relatively small cuts in military spending could lead to relatively enormous increases in funding for the arts with no effect on military security. Advocates for increased funding for nutrition and other human services have printed bumper stickers that ask "What if the government paid for day care, and the military held bake sales to buy guns?" The humor is a function of the extraparadigmatic perspective. In the current economic climate the military and the human services domains of government are experiencing funding cuts, but the values that determine funding decisions are unlikely to change.

The scientific paradigm examines facts as if they existed without context. As a result, when groups request that the facts be examined in context (social, cultural, economic) they are accused of confusing the issues or being special interest groups. They are clarifying issues by describing their complexity and suggesting a wider range of approaches. Changing the context may change the facts. Feeding infants may decrease the costs of special education years later. Improving the success rates in our schools may decrease the size of the prison population. Providing holistic support programs for at-risk students may increase the wages that are taxed for Social Security years later. All these approaches depend on seeing information in context and envisioning a very complicated process of unfolding events. None of these approaches makes sense if it is presented in strict cause and effect terms. The potential success of each depends on the attitudes of those who participate in implementing solutions. Individual attitudes such as optimism, faith, or belief in equal access are generally not measured when setting policy. The interpretive lens of positivism and objectivism do not present the most accurate picture when viewing complex problems that include hopes and fears as well as empirical data.

The American paradigm tends to frame significant differences as representing confusion, transition, or error. Two-valued logic requires that all data be assigned to rigid, mutually exclusive categories. As a nation of immigrants, our metaphor for acculturation in the 18th and 19th centuries was the melting pot, which was based on the eventual elimination of cultural differences. People who could adapt to the national paradigm could find a way to fit in by changing beliefs, behavior, diet, or physical appearance. People who could not or would not adapt because of unchangeable characteristics or because the cost of changing their paradigm was too high were excluded no matter how long they remained in the United States. English and Scottish immigrants, predominantly male, defined the American cultural paradigm in the earliest colonial days. They retained their own hierarchical social system, considered the Native people savages, construed African slaves as nonhuman, and presented their paradigm as objective reality. Jefferson and his peers considered darker skin to be prima facie evidence of natural differences between groups and possible illness as well (Takaki, 2008). These differences were extended to include a ranking of differential intelligence, passion, sensitivity, and capacity for the other supposed attributes of civilization. Rather than formulate a concept of Africans and Native Americans as people who lived differently with different spiritual beliefs, different ways to conceptualize family, and different methods of feeding, clothing, and interaction with other groups, the Founding Fathers considered these people less than human and developed means to subdue and dominate them. They used the lens of eugenics, which focuses on birth characteristics, rather than eunomics, which defines citizenship by participation in creation of a law-abiding society, as their guideline for determining citizenship (Hannaford, 1994). They thus created a lens in which race played a large part, and behavior, or other changeable aspects of a person, played a small part.

The scientific paradigm, which has taken American culture so far technologically, seems to have reached its limits in terms of its hegemonic status (Zakaria, 2008). The limits of this paradigm restrict our ability to understand or cope with the unprecedented cultural and economic diversity of the 21st century. Perceiving the world through this lens may cause a person of European ancestry to wonder how long a person with Asian features has lived in the United States even though the Asian family arrived 100 years earlier than the European family. It may cause us to wonder why children of Indian immigrants are still so resistant to eating hamburger or dating, or when Latino/Latina Americans are going to realize that young people should leave home after completing their education, or when immigrants from the Middle East are going to learn to be on time and get their business done efficiently without talking about their families or drinking tea.

Border Crossings and New Paradigms

In the 21st century the United States and its institutions of higher education are struggling to adjust to a world in which profound, apparently irreconcilable, differences can no longer be avoided. Large numbers of graduate and undergraduate students still come to the United States to study, but the Bologna Process (Gaston, 2010) is reframing European approaches to learning and attracting students who might previously have studied in the United States. Students from India and China often outnumber American students in engineering programs and come to the United States only to study not to migrate. Their motivation to enculturate is far less than that of their predecessors who studied in the United States and remained. We have reached the limits of the scientific paradigm as a frame of reference for coping with this cultural complexity. We have arrived at the border of the paradigm that so heavily influences American culture. Our students are studying abroad in increasing numbers and are being exposed to multiple perspectives through technology. They have easy access to global perspectives and easier access to video games that require mental agility and perspective shifting. We are moving across the border of the two-logic American paradigm without new maps for making sense of the new worlds we encounter. A step Americans must now take is to begin to understand the role of culture in shaping individuals. We must begin to experience the reality of people from many other cultures as a personal experience and go beyond intellectual understanding of other cultures presented in objective descriptions. From personal experience, I have seen the damage created by students who have learned about other cultures and never met members of those cultures. Their first encounters with those who are different are painfully marred by stereotypes and misunderstandings that can only be dismantled with careful mindfulness (Hanson, 2009; Siegel, 2007). We all must be willing to tolerate the confusion and discomfort that is inevitable as we cross the border from one view of the world to a world where many views coexist. We must move from domination to participation, from assuming that we set the standards to realizing that in this new world we should be contributing to their creation. Our universities need to shift emphasis to helping students understand category creation, among other things, and away from intellectual learning that does not challenge existing categories. The profession of student affairs whose members are exceptionally skilled in managing ambiguity and helping people learn to develop their own categories of analysis, can play a critical role in supporting this shift of emphasis from teaching what is known to helping people learn what they need to know.

PART TWO

SHIFTING INDIVIDUAL
PARADIGMS TO
EFFECT CHANGE

6

BORDERLANDS

Fear of the Other and Significant Differences

ote: This chapter marks a transition in this book. We are moving from the author's analysis of American culture and learning processes to the reader's experience of both phenomena. As a reader you are requested to begin cocreating your understanding and learning experience so you can begin to use what you know. The first step in this process is mindfulness, paying attention to your own experiences and reactions. The second step is articulation of your experiences, putting words to them. The third step is applying your new insights to your own behavior and understanding. The last step is also a first step. This is a circular process.

Situation

When I was in college I did some research at the New York Public Library's Schoemberg Collection, one of the premier collections of information about African Americans in the United States, located in Harlem. I went to the library on a Saturday morning. When I emerged from the subway it appeared to me that I was the only White person as far as the eye could see. I was terrified. The streets were filled with Black people doing their Saturday morning errands. Nobody paid any attention to me. I grew up with many Black friends and was intimately involved with several Black families. Why would I be frightened in Harlem? Certainly not because I am White, and everybody else was Black. I was afraid because they were all strangers, and I was totally ignorant about everything I needed to do that day. I had to ask directions to the library. I found it but didn't know how to use the closed stacks system. I had to be instructed. I felt like a White stupid person because everybody else in the library was Black, and they all seemed to know what they were doing. Being smart really matters to me. Being a strange, stupid White person in an alien world completely dislocated me from my familiar anchors. I was afraid to ask about places to eat lunch because that would have involved much more of my own ignorance and many more strangers. I went home to the Westchester suburbs as quickly as I could. I never discussed this incident with my Black friends because I was ashamed of myself.

If you are a White person, can you imagine yourself in this situation? If you are a person of color, how often have you been in comparable situations? No matter who you are, imagine a conversation in which you share your experiences. What are your thoughts? Your feelings? Why does it matter?

Fantasy (or Maybe Not)

Imagine you are a five-year-old living in a world where homosexual relationships are normal and heterosexual relationships are considered abnormal, sick, or sinful. You have either two moms or two dads and so does everybody else in your kindergarten. The teacher is a lesbian and talks about her life with her partner and their three children. Life feels pretty good to you in kindergarten because you can play with all the toys and learn whatever you enjoy and nobody tells you what's okay for a girl or a boy to do. Fast-forward to age 14, and some strange things seem to be happening to you. You want to spend more time with the opposite sex. You daydream about being really close to members of that sex. When you're around them you feel happy and you don't really care about dating members of your own sex. But you know that if you said anything to anybody, your parents, your teachers, your pastor or rabbi or imam, they would tell you that you were going through a phase, you would grow out of it, or that it was sinful and you should pray about it. People begin to suspect there's something strange about you. Some people even throw you up against your locker at school and accuse you of being "straight" or a "breeder." You start having trouble in school because you're afraid and can't concentrate. You consider suicide because you just can't stand how everybody is treating you. Your parents are worried about you but you can't really tell them what's going on.

If you are a straight person, how does it feel to imagine this world? If you are a gay, lesbian, bisexual, or transgender person, how would you feel in a world set up to see you as normal? Feelings really matter here. Take some time to pay attention to yours.

Differences and Fear

Why are differences so frightening to us? What do we know about our reaction to differences based on new information about preconceived ideas and neural architecture? Physiologically, any perception or experience that is dramatically unfamiliar to us, for example, rivers running in the wrong direction or water swirling counterclockwise as it goes down the drain, men kissing in public, or a four-year-old child with a smoking habit, all require us to make sense of the experience. Making sense of any experience requires us to perceive, interpret, place in personal context, and make decisions about actions that might be necessary. When experiences are familiar, such as getting ready for work in the morning, we go through them almost without thinking. The brain patterns are set up and in use. On a dress-down Friday, things are a bit more challenging because new patterns and rules are ambiguous. Why can we learn new languages in class and learn to write fairly well but have trouble speaking a new language? That is a complicated question, but the answer includes being afraid of sounding foolish and being afraid of not being understood. Even when speaking one's mother tongue, many people think of things they should have said in a stressful situation, long after the situation has passed. Fear makes understanding and doing what we want to do very difficult. We tend to be afraid of the unknown, particularly when facing the unknown requires us to say something or do something. That's a big part of the explanation why different groups eat lunch together in the school cafeteria. In your own peer group everybody knows what's expected, and nobody has to experience the discomfort that goes with not knowing. In new situations learning is required for success, and all learning involves emotion that runs along a continuum from pleasure to pain.

Borderlands and Crossings

The United States has always been a country of immigrants. Although large numbers of indigenous people in North America were here when the settlers/ conquerors arrived, many immigrants saw the Native people as barely human. They constructed their notion of Native people as the Other, a process that occurs when one group perceives another group to be so different from itself that the differences become extremely significant. The definers use the defined to draw the boundaries of their own humanity and group membership, in other words, to construct their identity. Since Native people were not Christian, did not have a banking system, had different family arrangements, and different ideas about land use and residences, the settlers defined them as uncivilized pagans. They created a category or lens that viewed Native people as totally and permanently Other. "As exiles living in the wilderness, far from civilization, the English used their negative images of Indians to delineate the moral requirements they had set up for themselves" (Takaki, 2008, p. 41). Most societies construct the Other to serve the purposes of the dominant group. The Other has come to signify "the negative of the socially affirmed self" (Kovel, 1984, p. 29). From a psychohistorical perspective, fear of the Other provides a reflection of the dominant group's fear of its own unacceptable impulses and desires. From a purely biological perspective, humans seem to be wired to care about "us" and reject "them" (R. Hansen, personal communication, January 8, 2001). Knowing who are members of one's own tribe has had survival value since the days of hunters and gatherers.

Given their propensity to look at physical phenomena for evidence of a natural or Divine order, the English simultaneously described differences between themselves and the indigenous people as natural and moral. These differences could and should not be overcome. The same logic was applied to Africans when they became slaves. "The English possessed tremendous power to define the places and people they were conquering. As they made their way westward, they developed an ideology of savagery which was given form and content by the political and economic circumstances" (Takaki, 2008, p. 44). Conquered people were treated as children, and the invaders considered themselves responsible for maintaining order in their new settlements. Since so many of the early immigrant groups intended to establish their own versions of the Kingdom of God, they believed they had a mandate to wipe out oppositional groups if those groups could not be civilized according to the immigrants' categories and definitions.

As North America was populated by Europeans, the assimilation process continued, suppressing differences among immigrant groups and encouraging the development of similarities. People who looked, spoke, and acted like the first immigrants had the easiest task of assimilating into colonial culture. To the degree that people looked different from northern European immigrants and spoke differently, that is, with accents, they found it difficult to be considered Americans regardless of the length of time they and their families had lived in the United States (Takaki, 2008). Race and physical appearance continue to be an American preoccupation. The question of what are you haunts children of biracial unions. Americans continue to create borders and categories based on physical appearance and behavioral characteristics and then to use those categories to decide who's in and who's out. Whenever a border must be crossed, learning is required, and that learning may be painful.

Cultural Pluralism and Multiple Borders

To this point culture has been defined as an ethnic phenomenon using common language, place of residence, religion, values, behavior patterns, and other cognitive categories as central characteristics. A broader definition of culture is

> an understanding that a people have of their universe—social, physical or both—as well as their understanding of their behavior in that universe. The cultural model of a population serves its members as a guide in their interpretation of events and elements within their universe; it also serves as a guide to their expectations and actions in that universe or environment. (Ogbu, 1990, p. 523)

Ogbu (1990) describes how cultures tend to produce folk theories of how the world works, based on the collective historical experience of the group. For example, the notion that you can't be academically smart and Black is currently a powerful folk theory among many young African American students in the public schools despite the presence of powerful Black intellectuals such as bell hooks, Bayard Rustin, Cornell West. and W. E. B. DuBois, in the United States since the mid-19th century.

Using Ogbu's (1990) description of culture, cultural groups can emerge from particular collective experiences in specific times and places and not necessarily involve a common ethnic background. The gay, lesbian, bisexual, transgender, questioning, intersex culture has been shaped by a common understanding of themselves as outsiders in a heterosexual world and common experiences of exclusion, harassment, invisibility, and other forms of oppression. Other cultural groups include people with disabilities, particularly the deaf, homeless, survivors of domestic abuse, members of age cohorts, veterans, and men and women (Howe & Strauss, 1993). The student affairs profession also shares some elements of a culture because of its historical outsider status in the academy (Fried, 1981, 2007; Lloyd-Jones, 1938), its set of identifiable values (Reason & Broido, 2011), the traditions and rites associated with national organizations and professional preparation programs (Dungy & Gordon, 2011), and its recognition of the borders between itself and other cultures in the academy. Using this expanded definition of culture, all people are members of multiple cultures, and all folk theories and explanations of a particular culture may be more or less salient for each person depending on the situation, time, and place (Abes, Jones, & McEwan, 2007).

Ogbu's (1990) definition of culture permits us to move beyond ethnicity and race to investigate culture as a created and very fluid phenomenon. Every time student affairs professionals serve on a committee that also includes faculty members, academic administrators, or students, those staff members bring cultural assumptions with them that guide their behavior. Student affairs professionals probably assume their ideas about student welfare should guide decision making, while faculty members may assume their ideas about departmental priorities or curricular issues are the most important. Students may have very different ideas of what they need for their own welfare, and their ideas are shaped by many factors, including gender, race, ethnicity, sexual orientation, religious involvements, and disability status.

The Intersection of Power and Culture

Culture cannot be discussed in isolation from the larger contexts it interacts with (Renn & Arnold, 2003). In situations where one culture exists within another or must engage with another regularly, power differences between the two must be taken into account to develop a comprehensive understanding of the situational dynamics. Power can be defined as the ability to advance one's goals and achieve one's ends in a particular social, political, economic, or cultural context. The group that has the most power in any context determines or heavily influences definitions of value, truth, good, justice, and other elements that affect social relationships. The dominant value system in the United States has been described previously. Groups that support nondominant values often have a great deal of difficulty getting equal time, equal respect, and fair treatment. The extended conflict over "Don't ask, don't tell" is one example of this type of conflict. Disputes about illegal immigrants and their status is another. What does fair mean in these conflicts? Without acknowledging the power issues in our efforts to understand diversity, the dominant group commits a serious affront to all nondominant groups. Diversity training without discussion of power involves "a notion of cultural critique that is largely limited to giving privileged Americans the benefits of cross-cultural knowledge" (Harrison, 1991, p. 5). Unfortunately, the vast majority of diversity training programs on campuses seem to lack the cultural critique Harrison refers to. Even at committee meetings, one must ask whose definitions of power and truth prevail when a university attempts to solve a problem. The foundational values are usually invisible or unacknowledged.

As we begin to create courses and programs that intentionally blend cognition, affect, and behavior, we must continuously ask whose values prevail. What knowledge is worth academic credit? Who is qualified to teach? Who decides? When power to dominate operates by defining knowledge and truth, validating some aspects of human experience and devaluing or ignoring others, it constitutes an extremely subtle and malignant form of oppression because it undermines people's confidence in their own ability to make sense of their world (Freire, 1994). This hegemony of meaning making can and does lead to self-hatred, lack of self-confidence, resentment, and hostility within groups and between the dominant and nondominant groups. People who are defined as Other in any culture often become resentful and relatively powerless. Historically, student affairs work has been defined as noneducational, and therefore the profession has often been treated as Other within the academy.

Question: How do you, the reader, feel when you read the assertion that student affairs professionals are one of the Others in the academy? Do you agree? Does it matter? From what perspective are you answering this question? If you are an academic with student affairs responsibilities, does this affect you in any way? Is there anybody you can discuss this experience with?

Americans have historically resisted thinking about power differences between groups, particularly class differences, because American mythology affirms the power of the decontextualized individual to achieve anything he or she wants to achieve (Bellah et al., 1985). Americans in the dominant culture seem to have a vested interest in blaming dominated people for their condition rather than looking at the context of their oppression. Research on the struggles of first-generation students (Allesandra & Nelson, 2005) has begun to erode this perspective in student affairs, but the national propensity to blame the victim is still widespread. Two-valued logic also contributes to the construction of this problem. Rather than viewing an individual in context, able to control some parts of his or her life and unable to affect others, many Americans see individuality and autonomy operating to the exclusion of contextual effects. Claude Steele's (Steele & Aronson, 1995) work on stereotype threat has provided powerful insight into the effect of context on intellectual achievement focusing on academic achievements of African Americans.

Perspective, Understanding, and Power Relationships

Question: Think about the situations in which you are usually a member of the dominant group, and other contexts in which you are an outsider. Does your perspective shift as context and power to affect circumstances shift? How does this process feel? Have you ever thought about it? Could you discuss it with anybody?

A person's perspective about events and their meaning is profoundly affected by the cultural groups that person belongs to and the salience of those groups in a particular situation. Questions emerge about which group has the power to establish definitions, categories, and truth values in that context. This approach to understanding culture, meaning, and hegemony reconfigures our understanding of the importance of perspective. Claims to universal truth and objectivity become questionable, misleading, disrespectful, and possibly dangerous (Harding, 1993). Harding refers to claims of objectivity as the "God trick" (p. 57). She asserts that the claim to objectivity and universal truth is part of the scientific belief system, or scientism. Fairness or impartiality cannot be achieved in her view, unless the perceiver/definer makes his or her standpoint and biases clear, a process she calls "the emerging logic of multiple subjects" (p. 2). Phenomena formerly believed to have objective, separate existences must now be considered as "a relation rather than a thing or an inherent property of people. Race, gender, ethnicity and sexuality do not designate any fixed set of qualities or properties of individuals, social or biological" (p. 2). Thus a complex understanding of human phenomena involves awareness of one's own standpoint and its biases, awareness of events described, and awareness of the interactions between them. This approach to understanding is far more complex than efforts to discern a singular, universal truth. Contributing to one's perspective and interpretation of events are the cultural lenses through which events are observed and the power differentials between various cultures and perspectives that interact in a particular situation. A poignant and painful example of this type of problem is that of initiation practices used by some historically Black fraternities. What does the symbolism of the chain and the brand mean to African American men? To White students? To university administrators? The meaning of these two symbols is very powerful. They are related to the historical experience of African slavery in the United States. Which group has the power to define the meaning of these symbols and explain their use to the community at large?

Even a person's understanding of who she or he is in a particular situation can change as events unfold (Abes et al., 2007). A dominating student leader, perhaps a pledge master in a fraternity, may harass pledges, act submissively with the chapter president, and be deferent but noncompliant with the Interfraternity Council adviser who is a woman and a member of the student affairs staff. An African American student may act and speak one way in a meeting of the Black student union and behave very differently when she serves on the president's advisory council for the college. Gay and lesbian students may behave differently at work and on campus for reasons of self-protection. Each of these situations evokes behavior that the person involved believes would be most effective to accomplish specific goals, and none of it defines the person in a rigid manner.

Border Crossings and Bifocal Perspectives

It is now apparent that most people, and certainly most Americans, are members of multiple cultural groups, and that perspectives shaped by different group memberships may be operative and conflicting in any given situation. Therefore, border crossings are intrapersonal processes in which any person might engage as the situation changes, and interpersonal processes that occur when members of one group have to do business with members of another group. Border crossings involve changes in understandings of events, in self-perception, and in power relationships. They are frightening, decentering, and fascinating. They operate differently for members of the dominant culture than they do for members of nondominant cultures.

Intrapersonal Borders

Question: Can you list at least 10 groups that affect your sense of identity, and identify places where membership in a particular group poses a problem in a particular context? For example, being female in an engineering class; being a student affairs professional at an academic department meeting; being the straight adviser to a lesbian, gay, bisexual, transgender, questioning student organization; or being "a one-legged man at a fanny kicking."

Intrapersonal borders emerge when people move from one setting to another, and a new aspect of their cultural background becomes salient. People from working-class backgrounds cross a border when they attend college or begin to work in a profession. The norm in working-class families is to think about work as providing hourly wages. Work is what you do to earn money but is rarely considered an intrinsic motivator. On the other hand, work among professionals carries intrinsic motivations, implies a service ethic, relevance to social values, and a shared culture. Professional work assumes continual, creative thinking about the ways the quality of one's professional work can be improved (Carpenter, 1991).

When race is the salient issue, as it often is in discussions of cultural diversity, Euro-Americans must move across an intrapersonal border from viewing White as the normal experience of humanity to viewing Black as another normal experience of humanity. White people must begin to transcend cultural stereotypes about race as well as their internalized racism, their fear of the Other, constructed around race. Given the racist heritage of the United States, when a White person seriously attempts to experience a Black person as fully human, that White person must reshape his or her identity and reconsider the relationship between race and identity. In a culture that prizes individuality and de-emphasizes group membership, this can be extremely frightening. Changing the relative importance of a significant element of one's individuality has the potential to cause disintegration among other less important elements.

The practice of border pedagogy has arisen as an approach to helping people make intrapersonal border crossings by "examining the conditions of their own existence" (Grossberg, 1994, p. 13). Students learn to step outside their own culture and examine how their ideas about themselves and others have been created by the culture—the media, the arts, religion, schooling, and so forth. These teachers use an approach called *interpretive rationality*, a process by which students are asked to examine how various differences are acknowledged and are ignored. Within the framework of the problematic approach, the meaning of events, the questions asked, and the questions that remain unasked become subjects of the discussion and inquiry (Giroux, 1981). Interaction between content and process, knowing facts, and creating meaning is explored. Typical questions might include: Why has race become such an important difference, and who benefits from this distinction? Why is physical appearance so important, and who does this construction serve? What do visible labels on clothing mean? Why does it matter if a woman chooses to cover all or parts of her face in public? A significant purpose of border pedagogy is to help people learn where borders have been established, explore the forces that established them, learn how each person is defined by the relevant borders, and whether people feel comfortable and competent within the borders that supposedly define them. Border pedagogy is intended to provoke transformative learning, the expanded awareness by learners of their own frames of references so they can move from frame to frame and appreciate multiple perspectives. Chapter 12 on intergroup dialogue describes pedagogies that support awareness and challenge. Read the following exercise, and pause to take time to think about your own ideas, attitudes, and opinions about Otherness.

Think of yourself as a person of another culture. If you are White, try thinking of yourself as African American; if you are African American, think of yourself as a member of an Asian culture or as a White American; if you are heterosexual, think of yourself as a person with a more fluid sense of sexual orientation. Try to make an inventory of your feelings and thoughts, what you might gain from the change and what you might lose. Continue this exercise for the next several weeks and keep a journal of your reactions. Place yourself in situations where people of another culture constitute the majority, and pay careful attention to your reactions. Notice your nondominant status. Go to an African American church, a Mass said in Spanish, a Buddhist temple, a mosque, or an orthodox Jewish synagogue. Go to cultural events sponsored by different groups, and pay careful attention to the similarities, the differences, and your reaction. Read novels and poetry by authors from groups that are different from yours. As you begin to see yourself and your group(s) as constructions of culture, you have begun your own border crossings.

This exercise is intended to help you discover your own borders. The process of border crossing itself pushes many Americans over another border. Suddenly reality is experienced as a construction that varies with individual perspective, not a condition external to and independent of the individual. This border crossing goes from positivist empiricism to subjectivist constructivism, a crossing of enormous significance. It involves the disorienting kind of learning described earlier. It takes awhile to internalize and an even longer time to put into action in one's personal behavior.

Border Crossings From Anthropology to Psychology

Border crossings have been described in the language of intellectual and moral development (Baxter Magolda, 1993; Kegan, 1994; King & Kitchener, 1994) as progress people make when they learn to infer meaning from context and organize data to support values and perspectives. When King and Kitchener discuss reflective judgment and wisdom, they are describing the elements of intellectual and moral development that permit people to manage the "unavoidable, difficult problems that are inherent in adult life, problems that do not have clear-cut solutions, where people need the ability to recognize the uncertainty of knowing and [possess] the ability to find shared meaning that allows wise judgment" (p. 219). In that process students learn the skills to untangle facts from meaning and realize on an emotional as well as intellectual level that all reality is not "out there." When students realize that construction of reality is a process they engage in daily, they become capable of crossing, creating, moving, or eradicating borders. They are able to differentiate between a range of perceived skin tones and the social construction of race and Otherness. Having visited their own internal borders, they can "go beyond the empty pluralism that always racializes the Other but never makes whiteness visible" (Giroux, 1994, p. 41). Teaching students how to engage in these deconstructive processes is called *border pedagogy*, which "decenters as it remaps" (Aronowitz & Giroux, 1994, p. 41), breaking down the dominant narratives that construct reality and often accepted unquestioningly by students, faculty, and administrators in higher education, just as it has been accepted by many Americans, particularly those who benefit.

The process of decentering and remapping discussed by Aronowitz and Giroux (1994) is internally frightening and disorienting. Siegel's (2007) description of neural architecture provides a biological basis for understanding the phenomenon Aronowitz and Giroux observed. Decentering and remapping is another way to describe deconstructing neural architecture, creating new neural pathways and biochemical, emotional responses for information that was previously known and now must be reinterpreted. Identity, which involves a particularly complex set of neural pathways and relationships, is constructed in relation to a particular social reality, another complex set of neurobiochemical responses. When the map of reality changes and is seen as a human construct, identity can be distorted or reshaped, possibly to the point of disintegration.

Questions: Who am I if I don't know who I am in relation to my environment, my friends, my goals, my family, and so forth? If my ideas about the permanence of Truth have been so disrupted that Truth is no longer stable, how do I know what knowledge to trust?

Perry (1968) described the continuous process of moving from a belief in an external Authority, which presumably conveys reliable knowledge, to a perception that there is no external Authority and to the realization that one must become one's own Authority/authority and live by one's self-chosen, contextually evaluated standards for truth. Transitions between perspectives often produce crises of identity. Perry's work on intellectual and ethical development described the border crossings of Harvard students in the 1960s and has become a classic work for student development educators. Progress along Perry's scheme of intellectual development allows people to become aware of perspective, to look within for the assumptions that shape perspective, and to loosen their hold on the search for absolute Truth or Authority. Higher levels of intellectual development as described by Perry permit understanding of "the logic of multiple subjects" (Harding, 1993, p. 2) and enable people to imagine the borders that can be crossed if they have the courage. Kegan (1994) and Baxter Magolda (1999) refer to this process as self-authorship, which implies autonomy and leads the way to "interpenetration of self and others" (Kegan, p. 314), a similar idea to Harding's logic of multiple subjects.

The process of making the initial border crossing from naive positivism to constructivism, from belief in Authority as given to authority as constructed and fluid, is different for members of the dominant cultural group in the United States than it is for other groups. Members of all other groups have to cross borders constantly. They do not have the luxury of believing that one standard fits all situations. Members of the dominant group are more likely to have this luxury because they are far less likely to need to adapt in foreign territory to survive, and they may not realize that other people are adapting to their expectations. Students of color who succeed on predominantly White campuses do so by learning appropriate behavior for the setting—how to behave in class, how to respond on tests, how to study, what to study, how to talk to White professors, and how to make friends with White students. To the degree that their upbringing has been shaped by different standards and expectations than those of their White peers, they know the way they act at school is learned behavior designed to bring them success in that environment. When gay and lesbian students don't talk about their personal lives or pretend they have intimates of the opposite sex, they know where the border is and when they have crossed it. When women leaders learn to talk about men's sports or cars, they have also crossed a border into a world of White male culture, and they know it. When student affairs professionals discuss cognitive or psychosocial student development with faculty members, they are opening doors for educators from other disciplines to cross into the cultural domain of student affairs. When they discuss the faculty member's scholarship, they have crossed the border in the opposite direction. When they talk about student behavior, they are wandering in a demilitarized zone and may not know where the border is. This particular subject has become increasingly important as student behavior in classrooms has become more of a problem. Student behavior is a very fertile area for creating dialogue across borders.

All nondominant groups must know where the borders are, because moving into the territory of the dominant group defines them as Other and subjects them to the likelihood of cultural erasure at best and violence or disrespect at worst. Members of the dominant group can remain oblivious to borders because their version of reality, value, and truth dominates wherever they are. They represent the hegemonic belief system even when they do not constitute the numerical majority. Through their domination of the major sources of ideological indoctrination in the country, the press, the church, the schools, the arts, and so forth, they validate their perspective and ignore or devalue others (Giroux, 1981). The hegemonic powers are currently shifting and being challenged on many fronts because of the wide accessibility of electronic communication and the Internet, but the challenges are a work in progress. The traditional, dominant perspective remains as the default for significant numbers of people. Examples of this default perspective in operation are (a) staff of an all-White department that can't find a "qualified" member of an Affirmative Action group because they can't differentiate between professional qualifications and their personal discomfort, (b) a psychology department dominated by positivist researchers who will not hire a person whose expertise is in qualitative research because the research is not "sufficiently rigorous," and (c) a curriculum committee that won't grant academic credit for a first-year experience course because it is too experiential, and they are not aware that experiential learning is a legitimate approach to pedagogy. The positivist paradigm is so pervasive in higher education that there are many sites where people are not even aware this paradigm is shaping decisions. Multiple perspectives or the logic of multiple subjects is not a part of the operating cognitive or affective systems.

Crossing Borders and Border Conflicts

Existentially, intrapersonal border crossings may be more difficult than interpersonal ones, but they are less visible and generally less violent. Interpersonal and intercultural border crossings are the ones we see daily on campus as we wonder why the Puerto Rican or Mexican students only eat with members of their own group, why there are so few men in women's studies courses, or why multicultural membership on the basketball and soccer teams is so unusual. The phenomenon of White students' hanging out with other White students rarely commands the same level of attention.

Two issues make intergroup border crossings a big problem in the United States. First, America lacks an ideology of legitimate difference associated with group membership. Americans do not have a language to discuss group differences in nonhierarchical, nonjudgmental ways. We are too enmeshed in judgments of worth, in cultural emphasis on individual autonomy, and too wedded to our historical ideology of the melting pot to value teaching our young people how to converse about group-related differences honestly (Mohanty, 1994). Fortunately this phenomenon is changing in many places but has not yet become widespread in areas where the population tends to be homogeneous. Chapters 9 through 13 in this book describe programs that teach students how to shift perspective and discuss differences, taking into account the cognitive, affective, and behavioral components of learning and change. At the present time many of us treat differences as family secrets. As with all family secrets, what is not discussed becomes a matter of shame, a matter of pretending the situation does not exist, a matter of confusion and dishonesty (Terkel, 1992). The historically accepted theories of racial, minority, and lesbian, gay, and bisexual identity formation reflect this concern because they correlate an individual's progress toward a positive sense of self with affirming or nonjudgmental acceptance of their own differences in comparison to identity formation in the dominant group (Atkinson, Morten, & Sue, 1979; Cross, 1978; D'Augelli, 1991). Within the various cultures created by students of color, numerous subdivisions are based on nonracial categories such as national origin, class, date of family migration, and primary language, which have received little attention in discussions of student culture. However, the lens distorts perception and leads to isolation of some groups from mainstream campus life because they perceive they are all being lumped together and not treated with respect or understanding.

How can we expect our students to understand cultural differences if they don't have the language and the confidence to discuss the issue, if there is no extensive public discourse about the content of the many different cultures that must coexist in this country? If we restrict these conversations to the various cultural celebratory months and weeks, members of the groups that are celebrated remain exotic Others. They are never seen by the dominant group as Americans who are college students, similar in many ways to themselves, people who are complete human beings entitled to act on their world, reflect on its problems, and transform it as they wish (Freire, 1970/ 1990). Cultural difference becomes entertainment rather than relationship— not a situation conducive to deepening intersubjectivity or mutual understanding.

Question: How does your campus handle multicultural programming? Do people "perform" for each other, or are they encouraged to explore the implications of their cultural differences in ongoing conversations? How comfortable are you in participating in such conversations? Are you a member of any group you do not feel comfortable discussing with people outside that group? What do you do about your own discomfort?

Most differences between groups involve power differences, which are a crucial part of cultural differences. A complete understanding of culture must include "antagonistic lived experiences" (Giroux, 1981, p. 27) within particular historical and social settings. These experiences involve the efforts of different cultural groups to make sense of their lives within the situation where cultures coexist and imply continual struggles to make power relations equitable among groups. Under the best of circumstances, groups strive for balance and equity. Under the worst, each strives for domination. Excellent portrayals of these kinds of conflicts appear in popular films such as *Freedom Writers* (DeVito, Shamberg, Sher, & LaGravenese, 2007) and *Crash* (Yari & Haggis, 2005), in which different groups compete for resources and domination of turf. *Freedom Writers* explores the journey from competition and domination to understanding and support, while *Crash* explores the impact of differing perspectives on people who must occupy the same space and address issues together without understanding each other's reality.

When exposed, power differences can easily provoke conflict. In any given situation the group with the greater power has the ability to define normal versus deviant, acceptable versus unacceptable, what's worth spending money on and what's not.

> The central issue, then, is not one of merely acknowledging difference; rather the more difficult question concerns the kind of difference that is acknowledged and engaged. Difference seen as benign variation (diversity) for instance rather than as a conflict, struggle or the threat of disruption, bypasses power as well as history to suggest a harmonious, empty, pluralism. (Mohanty, 1994, p. 146)

The majority of the public discourse on the "Don't ask, don't tell" policy in the U.S. military has been an example of unexplored conflict, characterized by assertions of belief that often contradict the data. The contradictions are rarely explored in depth, and despite the passage of legislation for the military, the conflict remains unresolved in large areas of our culture.

The majority of diversity education programs on American campuses seem to treat difference as empty pluralism, as if there were no history of differences. The history of difference in the United States is long and painful. Failure to acknowledge this denies the context that continues to give rise to difference. It also contributes to the inability of many Americans to perceive the consequences of these problems or feel responsible for addressing them. For example, African Americans came here as prisoners, large numbers of Japanese Americans were interned in concentration campus during World War II, many Catholics believed Jews were responsible for killing Christ until the Pope instructed Catholics to give up this belief, the White power structures in the Northeast and Southeast United States permitted great violence to occur during integration, many Korean Americans today are frightened for the safety of their families every time there is some sort of tension in dozens of ethnic ghettos in the United States, there are more Black men between the ages of 18 and 25 in prison than in college, Muslims in the United States have been increasing targets of violence to the extent that many feel as if their religious freedom is being eroded. These are group problems related to group perspectives, not individual difficulties.

Americans seem particularly unwilling to discuss differences in power between groups.

> The idea of freedom has historically given Americans respect for individuals. . . . but it is an idea of freedom that leaves Americans with a stubborn fear of acknowledging the structures of power and interdependence in a technologically complex society dominated by giant corporations and an increasingly powerful state. (Bellah et al., 1985, p. 25)

America lacks a history of awareness of class struggle with the exception of the early labor movement. Our history has been one of economic opportunity for so many people that our belief in the unlimited potential of the individual to succeed economically has, until the crash of 2008, not been seriously challenged in past generations. Michael Moore in his book *Stupid White Men* (2001) and subsequent films, has begun to expose the class structure for the general public. The wiki leaks and phone hacking scandals will certainly make class and economic conflict more apparent. Howard Zinn in his many editions of *A People's History of the United States* (e.g., see Zinn & Arnove, 2004) has also done a great deal to describe class conflict throughout American history, but still little is said about economic and class conflict in the public discourse.

Discussions of inequalities among groups in a democracy pose a problem. They carry the assumption that if one talks about them, to be fair, one is obligated to do something about them. Some power differentials among groups are now being adjudicated in the courts via class action lawsuits filed over equal treatment by sex, occupational and safety protections, voting rights, tenant rights, discriminatory dress codes, and access to single-sex educational institutions. These are examples of efforts to redress historical differences in power that have placed certain groups at a disadvantage. Redress for historical injustice has been extended legislatively to a certain extent to indigenous people regarding land rights and to Japanese Americans who were harmed by internment during World War II. All these civil actions acknowledge that some groups have had more power than other groups in the United States. These acknowledgments provoke discomfort because they deny the national mythology of equal opportunity for all, autonomy for the individual, and the irrelevance of history in shaping life experience. They decenter the American cultural map and shine spotlights on its borders.

Discussing power differences between groups almost certainly provokes conflict as well. In a system that pretends to promote equality, power differences ought to be temporary and subject to elimination. In a system of majority rule, whoever is in the minority simply cannot have equal opportunity to affect policy. In a student programming board that uses majority rule, the chances of a nondominant group getting enough money to stage a major event by itself is often quite small, not necessarily because of malevolence but because of competition for limited resources and the need to provide programming for the greatest number, the hegemonic group. How can we remediate historical inequalities in using the principle of majority rule when the majority does not generally give up its privileges voluntarily? De Tocqueville (1835/1956) called this phenomenon the *tyranny of the majority.*

Intergroup differences in developing campus programs are often suppressed because of the fear that they may also provoke conflict. Groups with an identity in their title such as African American Business Students or Women Engineers or particular services for lesbian, gay, bisexual, and transgender students, often evoke comments like, "Where's the White student union?" When students from similar backgrounds want to live together in residence halls they cannot exclude students from other groups de jure, but they are accused of de facto segregation. Seeing this issue from the perspective of members of nondominant groups, it is fairly easy to understand why students might want relief in their living quarters from students who drink to excess, are uncomfortably loud or listen to music that is offensive, or from students who don't pray three (Orthodox Jews) or five times (Muslims) a day. They might want to avoid people they don't know very well, yet who feel free to ask them personal questions about grooming, dress, eating habits, and male/female relationships. The issue is not simply one of separatism or discrimination but one of focusing on the perspective that defines the "problem" in the first place. Reframing definitions of problems implies shifts in power relationships, a process that is inevitably uncomfortable. The group entitled to define phenomena that are considered a problem is inevitably the group with the most power. Group power is a taboo topic. Discussing taboos requires us to dismantle our cognitive maps about the way the world works. Nobody wants to do it because it's just too confusing.

Border Blockades

Why don't we have more successful, spontaneous border crossings? Border crossings generally involve confusion, shifting power relationships, and a vague inability to understand how to achieve ones' goals and feel competent in the new situation. Dismantling cognitive maps leaves people confused because familiar connections may no longer be present. When border crossings are complicated by fear of the Other, a belief that the dominant, familiar way is the normal way and the other ways are not, it is difficult to care about the other group's interests and needs as much as you care about your own.

Some difficulties are directly related to the age or life circumstances of the students. Students are still faced with the developmental dilemmas of learning to manage their emotions and develop competence (Chickering & Reisser, 1993). They must learn to develop good decision-making strategies as they experience emotional pressure from impulses such as sex, aggression, anxiety, fear, guilt, and shame. Students' lives have become much more complex because of societal changes, economic changes, and the increased family responsibilities many students bring to college. When students are attempting to manage large debt burdens, the expenses of daily life, crowded classes, and an insecure job future, they probably don't have a lot of energy left to seek out uncomfortable situations in their time on campus or to make friends with strangers whose behavior makes them uncomfortable and who represent competition for jobs after college (Howe & Strauss, 1993). Under these circumstances, if students have time to make friends on campus they will probably seek out people who are similar to them and with whom they feel comfortable.

Administrators may make efforts to encourage intergroup activity, but intergroup dialogue is as difficult for them as for the students (see Chapter 12). These activities may provoke conflict or be disruptive or embarrassing to the institution. They can force administrators to rethink business as usual or to frame an issue from an unfamiliar perspective. Border crossings highlight differences between student and institutional perspectives and challenge the status quo. Legal responses are often ineffective, as demonstrated by the continuing inability of campus administrators to write speech codes that simultaneously protect freedom of speech and preserve an individual's right to be free from harassment.

Now What?

Honest border crossings in which one group of people who see the world from a particular perspective attempt to understand and negotiate with another group of people might reorder the foundations of higher education, and that would be very disruptive for everybody involved. People with more power would be obligated to see the world from the perspective of people with less power and to step outside their perspective of benevolent authority. Angry people would have to step outside their anger and try to understand the fear their anger engenders in others. White Americans would have to consider the benefits of whiteness and the implications of real Affirmative Action, experiencing the losses and the gains. Faculty members would have to make efforts to understand the students' lives and learning processes, splitting their focus between subject matter and relationships with their students. Many of them would have to reconsider their ideas about academic rigor and legitimate learning.

Student affairs administrators would have to give up their perceptions of problem students as Others, people who somehow need to be controlled to avoid professional embarrassment. They would have to develop relationships with students that manifest caring and control in a mutually respectful way (Noddings, 1988). They would have to cross the border from fear to courage and compassion when dealing with angry students and be willing to examine the system for procedures that might be unfair to groups. Simultaneously, they would have to attempt to understand the university from the perspective of many other groups and have equally strong vested interests in community welfare and the teaching/learning process. These other groups often behave differently and make decisions from different perspectives because they have different roles in the institution. All of us would have to replace blaming the Other with trying to understand multiple priorities, perspectives, and experiences. This is a move beyond diversity to the creation of a civil community in which conflict is acknowledged and addressed, in which differences are respected even in the absence of agreement, and students, faculty, and administrators share power in pursuit of common goals whenever possible. This process is border crossing, and it requires powerful learning in the mind, the heart, and in daily behavior and skill. This type of learning requires border pedagogy. Learning in this manner is essential to the recreation of higher education for the citizens of our democracy and for bringing civility back to public discourse.

The process is difficult, but it does have its rewards as described in an e-mail I received from a female student of Jewish and Christian descent in a multicultural counseling course:

> I could not wait until Tuesday to tell you what an amazing experience we had today at the mosque. We were greeted with such a warm and hospitable welcome, and the women were so friendly and open with us. Many of them came over to give us a hug, kiss, or handshake and sat down to talk with us. We observed the prayer and afterwards they announced us as visitors and encouraged everyone to come say hello. They styled our scarves as they wear their hijabs. Every detail of the visit was the exact opposite of how I pictured it being (that was the point, right?). We even exchanged phone numbers and emails to keep in touch with some of the women. This visit was a true definition of a life changing moment for me. I can't emphasize enough what a positive and meaningful experience it was—thank you for this assignment!

7

BORDER PEDAGOGY

From Teaching to Learning

B order pedagogy has been used to describe the process of helping people learn to consider new and disorienting ideas, particularly those that challenged their notions of self, power, and relationships (Fried & Associates, 1995; Giroux, 1981). Border pedagogy can also be understood as a significant teaching approach in experiential education. Learning how to cross borders is done most effectively through experiential learning using the action/reflection cycle (Kolb, 1984). In fact, there is no other way to learn how to cross borders because border crossing involves the kind of learning that engages all areas of the brain. Border crossing requires people to learn with their intellect and their emotions while simultaneously developing new behavior patterns and finding ways to make sense of the entire experience. Learning to cross borders successfully provides us with a comprehensive example of the complexity of learning processes, whether we are learning about intergroup differences or differences in philosophical perspectives.

The foundation of student affairs, more specifically of student development education, is experiential learning. Since Esther Lloyd-Jones (Lloyd-Jones & Smith, 1954) described student personnel work as *deeper teaching*, members of the student affairs profession have struggled to find terminology to describe the educational work we do with students. One answer to this problem has been hidden in plain sight for many years, and the time has come to explore the issue. Dewey (1916) called his philosophy of education *pragmatism*. Pragmatists emphasize the role of the mind as highly active in the creation of patterns and relationships found through examining data.

Problem definitions arise from the perception or creation of patterns that seem confusing or incomprehensible. Pragmatism emphasizes the experimental character of empirical science and elevates the role of the mind as the "active capacity for generating ideas whose function is to resolve the problems posed to an organism by its environment" (Scheffler, 1965, p. 5). Pragmatism combines positivism and constructivism into one flowing process.

Dewey spent the majority of his career examining the relationship between educational philosophy, educational psychology, and the need to prepare students to become effective citizens of our democracy. He asserted that "education is a constant reorganizing or reconstructing of experience. . . . [whose] is to add to the meaning of that experience [and] increase the ability to direct the course of subsequent experience" (1938, p. 89). Dewey emphasized the interaction between people and their environment, describing the processes by which people use to transform the environment as they learn about it, thus expanding their ability to learn. Dewey refused to be trapped in either/or thinking as it applies to the relationship between theory and experience.

> Experience is primarily an active/passive affair; it is not primarily cognitive. . . . The measure of the value of the experience lives in the perception of the relationships or continuities to which it leads up. It includes cognition in the degree to which it is cumulative or amounts to something or has meaning. . . . The separation of mind from the direct occupation with things throws emphasis on things at the expense of relations or connections. (pp. 164, 167)

Dewey's pragmatism is a process-oriented approach in which life becomes a laboratory and every person a scientist. Truth is considered a function of the interaction between the person who knows and that which is known. Truth is directly related to the context in which it is discerned and is modifiable as context, value, and meaning change via the person who discerns. Dewey's language antedates constructivism. It prefigures knowledge developed by the new science about connections and relationships (Wheatley, 1999) and current knowledge of neurological learning processes.

Dewey's insights were precursors to the knowledge about learning that has developed through the work of cognitive scientists and brain-based and experiential educators (Caine et al., 2005; Kolb, 1984; Zull, 2002). From his direct observation of his own learning processes and the ways children learned in various settings, he described what cognitive scientists are now able to observe in functional magnetic resonance imaging (fMRI) scans. Learning is an integrated process that occurs throughout the brain. It depends completely on the connections made between sensory and cognitive inputs, emotional responses to those inputs, and continuous rewiring of the neural structures that permit the individual to comprehend and apply the new information.

Historically, pragmatism has been considered one of three major approaches to education. The other two schools of thought that have dominated academic understanding of learning are *rationalism* and *empiricism*. Rationalism hypothesizes the existence of self-evident truths and assumes that reliable knowledge can be derived from these truth principles using deductive logic. Euclidian geometry is the most well-known example of this approach. Empiricism forms the foundation for the scientific method, which is largely unquestioned as the source of reliable information in the Western world. Empiricism considers reliable knowledge to be founded on observations of data. The goal of empirical research is to observe and describe data to generate principles, which yield reliable predictions over the widest possible field of data. Both of these approaches assume the separation of the observer from the observed and value the creation of increasing approximations of an ultimately static truth. Dewey and the cognitive scientists give far more emphasis to the role the mind plays in shaping meaning and reframing neural associations. They have a more dynamic understanding of learning than either of the other two schools of thought. Ironically, cognitive scientists have used empiricist methods to demonstrate the accuracy of Deweyan observations. Cognitive research on learning has crossed a challenging border, using the tools of the dominant scientific paradigm to document the functioning of a dynamic interactive world where connections and interactions create relationships that are more fundamental to reality than things.

What is the explanation of learning that has been hiding in plain sight? Belief systems and preconceived ideas frame the interpretation of information. What we think we know is generally shaped by what we expected to find through the learning process. Kuhn (1996) has documented the political nature of scientific interpretation and the difficulty of challenging widely accepted paradigms even when empirical evidence that contradicts the dominant paradigm accumulates. We do not change what we think we know based merely on new information. If we were able to make those kinds of changes based on information alone, the HIV epidemic would have stopped years ago and few smokers would ever pick up a cigarette. Learning is far more complex than hearing and repeating new information. When learning is expected to change belief systems or behavior, the process is difficult, complicated, and time consuming. The rationalist and empiricist epistemologies that dominate the academy do not acknowledge the influence of interpretation or emotions on perception. Neither do they permit us to discover unchanging Truth. They are valuable ways of understanding our logical and empirical worlds, but they are not the only ways. The constructivist logic of multiple subjects is our current reality, and one example of that reality is learning to understand diverse perspectives generated by cultural differences.

We are now crossing borders with the speed of light—borders between ethnic groups, between science and other ways of knowing, and between the belief in the possibility of objectivity and the belief that dialogue that acknowledges multiple subjectivities may provide the best insight into our common condition. We have entered an era when there are so many competing interpretations of the truth there is often no way of agreeing on empirical accuracy. The debt ceiling crisis provides an excellent example where all participants have access to the same economic data yet view the data through radically different perspectives, making agreement on solutions extremely difficult. On a much simpler level, there is no way of agreeing on empirical accuracy among four eye witnesses to a traffic accident if each witness was standing on a different street corner when the accident occurred. Students multitask constantly, taking notes in a lecture hall and simultaneously reading text messages, playing games, and checking the scores of their favorite teams. Each activity requires attention to information and the use of at least one interpretive perspective. Anyone who has attempted to resolve a roommate conflict knows that truth, or even accuracy, is often an illusion, and the best we can hope for is consensus and agreement on next steps. We have entered an era of unavoidable constructivism because of the existence of so many perspectives and our ability to know that these perspectives exist. The dominant empiricist paradigm (i.e., seeing is believing) is itself under significant challenge. Even the notion of self as a stable sense has been challenged (Abes et al., 2007). We have evolved to a level of awareness in which human beings are capable of seeing our interpretations of events, our belief systems, and our values as constructs. Many people believe their particular set of constructs constitute the truth, but many others live in a world where the influence of perspective on perception is acknowledged (Kegan, 2000; Zakaria, 2008). We are in a stone and pitcher situation, in a world of consensual reality where we may or may not agree on what information is considered to be factual, and all empirical knowledge is tentative. Nevertheless, the stone still has more power than the pitcher. We still privilege empirical knowledge in our daily lives, in our policy making, and in most other dimensions of human experience in the Western world. The bottom line for anything still presumably consists of numerical data, and feelings are considered less reliable than facts as a source of decision making. So if we do not always agree on what constitutes a fact, what do we mean when we talk about learning? What are the implications of this question for all the high-stakes standardized tests students are subjected to? What is the future of the "objective" test and the bubble sheet? Is this purely a philosophical question, or are there economic, political, and pedagogical ramifications? The answer to all this is yes.

Borders Everywhere and Not Crossing Them Is Impossible

New understandings of the interaction of cognition, affect, behavior, and meaning making render previous borders permeable if not illusory. Students learn everywhere on campus and in the other domains of their lives (Keeling, 2004). As they move through their college experience they tend to learn new ideas in one location, typically the classroom, and develop new emotional patterns and behavioral skills in other locations, typically outside the classroom. Often the brain takes care of putting ideas together with feelings and behavior, and the result is one of those wonderful aha moments we all love to see. Unfortunately, the structure of campus life does not place enough emphasis on this kind of integrated learning.

In colleges and universities where the distinction between academic affairs and student affairs is embedded in the organizational structure, holistic or transformative learning tends to occur by accident. To integrate living and learning, academic faculty and student affairs professionals must help students make connections. Faculty should ask students about the implications of their learning in the rest of their lives, and student affairs professionals must take time to point out the connections between learning that occurs in training programs, residential experiences, or disciplinary processes, and information students are learning in their courses. Service-learning provides an ideal integrated model, since reflection on experience is generally part of the process of learning. Engaging in service, reflection on personal experience and meaning, and placing the entire action/reflection process into a disciplinary or historical context is an excellent example of holistic, transformative learning where borders are intentionally acknowledged and crossed (see Chapter 10). If students do not make the connections between living and learning, they will probably not remember much of what they learn in class or know why they need to know it. They will also not be able to articulate what they have learned in various student life experiences. The border between living and learning must be crossed for students to develop self-authorship (Baxter Magolda, 1999) or to be able to examine and reframe their own values (Kegan, 2000). In many ways, border crossing is an excellent way to describe the educational mission of the student affairs profession. Students must make connections between what they learn cognitively and experientially to develop a sense of identity (Chickering & Reisser, 1993). For example, if students are to develop a sense of personal vocation, they must be able to reflect on their own talents, skills, and interests and place that configuration of knowledge into a context of meaning making and economic necessity for themselves and their community. Otherwise they are simply choosing a major and looking for a job.

Border crossings are also inevitable if students make friends or learn to work with people from different ethnic, racial, or religious backgrounds. If they get to know people from groups previously unfamiliar to them or groups they have only known through media presentations, they will inevitably have to change their opinions about specific members of those groups, their new friends, and colleagues. They are also very likely to change their own ideas about their personal identity, which is particularly true in racial and religious contexts. If a student has never thought about being White and has always assumed that Black people are poor or lazy or ignorant, then what does that individual do when he or she meets a smart Black person from a wealthy family? Does the presence of the other student have implications for the White student's sense of self? If a student believes Christianity is the one true faith, what does he or she do after realizing that Islam shares many beliefs with Christianity? What does this knowledge do to his or her own image as a Christian? To cross these borders, students must manage their emotions, develop the skills necessary to remain in uncomfortable situations, and if they are really interested, study more of the history and cultural practices of the different groups.

Research seems to indicate that the ability to cross these kinds of borders is directly related to being aware of one's own lenses and being able to shift lenses as necessary. "Cultural or personality differences are rarely the source of interpersonal or inter-group conflict. The most common source is what might be called 'mindsets,' filters through which people view the world, self and others" (Manning, 2003, p. 20). Differences among people do not seem to present as much of a barrier as internalized opinions of what those differences mean and whether a person has the courage to deconstruct preconceived ideas about meaning and self. Therefore, crossing borders between people who hold significantly different worldviews is inevitably disorienting. When that process is managed well, it becomes a holistic, transformative learning experience.

A Rigid and Invisible Border

The border between rationalist and empiricist epistemologies and pragmatist epistemology is profound. The first two philosophies frame what we traditionally consider learning in higher education. These traditions assume separation between a subject who thinks and observes, and an object that is thought about or observed. These epistemologies assume unidirectional relationships. Neither tradition assumes interaction or mutual shaping that occurs when students learn new information, or participants in a situation attempt to learn what they need to know to solve a problem. In the pragmatist/constructivist tradition, there is constant mutual shaping between agent and object, the knower and the known. The person engages with aspects of the environment to effect a change. A change occurs (or does not occur). The person thinks about the events and their significance and either persists in the course of action or changes direction. Events that occur subsequent to the action shape the pragmatists' ideas about what is desirable, what should happen next, and the utility or value of the desired ideas, and the process continues in an endless loop.

The border between rationalist/empiricist epistemologies and pragmatic epistemology exists in each person's understanding of the relationship between people and their environment—either as disembodied outsiders who manipulate and organize or embodied participants engaged in a dynamic, somewhat unpredictable, process of learning and growth. In the first case, emotions interfere with learning. In the second case, they are part of learning. In the two older traditions, rationalism and empiricism, knowledge is most valuable when it is most general, formal, or theoretical. In pragmatism, knowledge can be equally valuable and reliable when it provides accurate insight into the particular and personal. In the first case, valid knowledge is about the outside world, and personal knowledge is a distraction. In the second, knowledge is a combination of understanding the engagement between external and internal factors. In commenting on the subject/object split that pervades Western epistemology, Krishnamurti proposed the following synthesis:

> *First* you are a human being. . . . *then* you are a scientist. First you have to become free and this freedom cannot be achieved through thought. It is achieved through meditation—the understanding of the totality of life in which every form of fragmentation has ceased. (as cited in Capra, 1982, p. 29)

In other words, the subject/object split does not have to be construed as a split. It can be construed as a dynamic synthesis in which each aspect of a phenomenon contributes to the understanding of the other elements and the whole. The subject/object split is a creation of human thought, a set of categories used to understand the world. Another way to imagine this particular border is to see it as a set of neurological pathways (Siegel, 2007) that functions as a filter to place new information into well-established conceptual filters. Siegel and Krishnamurti suggest that meditation is one way to become aware of the categories created through the use of these pathways, not simply to dismantle them but to become aware of the ways they shape perception, opinion, and conclusions. When people become aware of the filters they are using to give meaning to perceptions, they enhance their own sense of self-authorship and realize they can be the meaning makers in their own lives. Categories and definitions are seen as the creation of conscious processes rather than as externally existing phenomena people apprehend and apply.

This border provides us with an understanding of our inability to see student affairs work as the deeper teaching and our difficulty in explaining the connection between experiential learning and academic teaching/learning. Student affairs professionals attended traditional colleges and universities. We, along with all our educated peers, have been trained to think of teaching as talking and showing and learning as repeating and imitating. We have been immersed in rational and empiricist pedagogies without even understanding or being aware of the philosophies that informed the teaching methods. Hidden in plain sight is the pragmatist approach to teaching and learning, which characterizes all the educational work done by student affairs professionals with students and often with colleagues.

Our roots in pragmatism are generally invisible. In fact, pragmatism as an educational approach is not widely understood or even talked about in professional discourse. W. H. Cowley talked about the student personnel perspective, the educational philosophy of student personnel, as

> a philosophy of education which puts emphasis upon the individual student and his all-around development as a person rather than his intellectual training alone and which promotes the establishment in educational institutions of curricular programs, methods of instruction and extra instructional media to achieve such emphasis. (as cited in Rentz, 1993, p. 69)

Cowley observed that his definition had two parts, the underlying emphasis, or philosophy, and the approaches and techniques that expressed the emphasis, or point of view. Cowley alluded to pedagogy when he suggested that student personnel work needed its own curriculum and methods of instruction, but that suggestion has not received widespread attention in language that is comprehensible to rationalist and empiricist faculty. Cowley (1936/1993) and Esther Lloyd-Jones (Lloyd-Jones & Smith, 1954) believed that those in the student personnel profession, as it was then called, needed to articulate and promulgate a philosophy of education as part of professional efforts to make the work understood in the wider community of higher education. The first official definition of the student personnel profession in the *Student Personnel Point of View* (American Council on Education, 1937), asserted that

> one of the basic purposes of higher education is the preservation, transmission and enrichment of the important elements of culture—the product of scholarship, research, creative imagination and human experience. It is the task of colleges and universities so to vitalize this and other educational purposes as to assist the student in developing to the limits of his potentialities and making his contribution to the betterment of society. (as cited in Rentz, 1993, pp. 67–68)

This is clearly a description of pragmatist education, but the broader foundation of this approach is never named or explicitly discussed.

Pragmatism as an approach to education is not widespread in colleges or universities. Empiricism and rationalism dominate pedagogy, policy, and management. They are both taken for granted and invisible. Therefore when student affairs professionals describe student learning by discussing training programs, changes in student behavior and understanding from the beginning to the end of a college career, or the transformative effects of a provocative dialogue on improving relationships between groups, these experiences are dismissed as anecdotal, meaning that the information is valid only in the specific situation and not generally applicable to large groups of students. Since our profession has not clearly described its philosophy of education, we have not been able to reframe the categories of interpretation that define learning. When Afrocentric philosophers challenged the dominant pedagogies and interpretive frameworks in the academy, they were able to create space for dialogue that included their perspectives (Appiah, 2006; West, 1993a). By describing her vision of Nguzo Saba, the seven principles of Kwanzaa, as part of an overall vision of student identity development, Johnson (2002) created an alternate view of what is considered to be normal development for African American students. The profession of student affairs has yet to create a framework for discussing its educational role and pedagogy in the academic world and is therefore not able to take its place in discussions of academic policy making because it remains an Other.

Earlier we discussed the need to make whiteness visible in discussions of race. When whiteness is not made visible, it is taken to be the normal condition of humanity, and people who do not appear White or come from European backgrounds are considered culturally diverse. In not acknowledging whiteness, the circumstance of European ancestry is privileged, unexplored, and invisible, and that lens shapes the interpretation of events. In not acknowledging empiricist and rationalist pedagogies, we privilege their interpretations of reality and are not able to create a dialogic space for pragmatist philosophy or pedagogy. The subject/object split epistemologies have defined the experience of academic learning since the creation of modern universities and therefore have the power and ability to discount personal learning as anecdotal and insignificant. It is time to claim the logic of multiple subjects for the experience of learning and to broaden our understanding of learning to include the results of student affairs work with students.

Pragmatist Pedagogy Doesn't Look Like Teaching

All border crossings are disorienting. Border crossings that reframe entire worldviews are tremendously uncomfortable and likely to provoke great resistance. The border crossing, even the process of making the border visible between rationalism/empiricism and pragmatism, will provoke great discomfort in the academy. As the culture wars of the 1980s dismantled and reframed the traditional canon of dead White males, not excluding their work but placing it in a much broader context of global culture, the inclusion of pragmatism as philosophy and pedagogy will have the same disruptive effect on conversations about teaching and learning.

> Borders are lines that are not neutral, that separate worlds not perceived as equal. . . . When borders are present, movement and adaptation are frequently difficult because knowledge and skills in one world are more highly valued and esteemed than those in another. (Phelan et al., 1993, p. 53)

The skills and knowledge of members of the student affairs profession are typically quite different from those of academic faculty. The first border crossing required to make pragmatist pedagogy visible is the creation of a common language about teaching and learning. Academic faculty tend to discuss content when describing learning, that is, what do the students need to know? Student affairs professionals tend to discuss process and skills, that is, what do the students need to be able to do or understand? Now we must ask what faculty members and student affairs professionals need to know about teaching and learning and content and process to create integrated learning environments? This will be a very long conversation. However, if this conversation is not undertaken, the continuing efforts of the student affairs profession to describe our work as education will not succeed because our pedagogy does not conform to traditional descriptions of teaching. In attempting to cross this border, we have less power. We do not create the categories of value. We remain the Other.

This conversation closely resembles a cross-cultural dialogue between academic faculty and student affairs professionals that generates a pragmatist process of creating mutual understanding between these two groups about teaching and learning. Academic culture and student affairs culture are quite different, and the differences must be negotiated in the same manner one would use in learning to live in a different culture (Fried, 1981). We must learn what we each believe about teaching and learning, what skills are required to help students learn, and how we will define learning outcomes we have confidence in. This dialogue is best approached by raising questions, comparing answers, and finding common ground. To equalize power issues, the conversations will be most effectively led by equals, probably people with terminal degrees in their fields. The conversation about teaching and learning is one that now incorporates multiple subjectivities and challenges the dominance of any singular approach to defining legitimate learning. Skill in managing a group process is essential for the success of these dialogues. Student affairs professionals teach students about group process constantly. This is one of our areas of expertise, and using it in the context of teaching/learning conversations would be an excellent place to begin (see Chapter 12).

Because student affairs remains the Other in academic environments where the governing philosophical paradigms are unacknowledged, the dialogue process is also a political process. *Critical consciousness,* a notion that Paulo Freire (1970/1990) introduced in his work to help Brazilian peasants become literate provides a template that can serve the student affairs profession well as an interpretive device in this dialogue. We need to become more literate in reading the academic elements of our environments. Critical consciousness is the process of helping people see themselves in context and read messages their environment sends them about who they are or ought to be and how they should interpret events. Critical consciousness helps people learn to read and label their world, describing and understanding events from their own perspective as shaped by race, class, gender, sexual orientation, religion, and ethnic culture. Critical consciousness is developed through *praxis,* a process of action and reflection in which people engage in efforts to understand and transform their world to make it more just and to achieve greater self-direction and dignity. In the student affairs/faculty dialogue another purpose is to transform ideas about teaching and learning to make them more effective and comprehensive.

To initiate praxis, or intentionally reflective conversations about transformative learning, student affairs professionals need to use their own cross-cultural competence to understand faculty culture. The messages the academy has sent to student affairs have focused heavily on work outside the classroom. That language highlights the one-down status of student affairs work and presumes without saying that outside the classroom means not learning, or at least not learning anything that has to do with academic learning. We need to ask ourselves what Freire would do in our situation. He would ask his peasant students to describe the environment that has discounted them or told them that their work was less significant than the work of the landowners. Then he would help them describe their circumstances from their own point of view and begin to change the way they relate to the landowners so that they see themselves holding valid, albeit different, perspectives on events and decisions. Finally he would suggest that dialogue begin in order to reframe the situation. For members of the student affairs profession, this means becoming familiar with the philosophical roots of our teaching/learning methods and being able to discuss philosophy and practice with faculty members whose approaches are different.

Higher Education Is Transforming as We Speak

There has not been a better time to initiate this dialogue in recent memory. Higher education is being critically examined from many perspectives, including cost, access, social/economic utility, value, and effectiveness. *Declining by Degrees: Higher Education at Risk* (Public Broadcasting Service & Merrow, 2005) describes the struggles students and faculty face in teaching and learning at all kinds of colleges, and questions the ability of students to learn under the circumstances of their lives. *Academically Adrift* (Arum & Roksa, 2011) documents the limitations of learning on college campuses, using the positivist research methods we have learned to respect and trust. Arum and Roksa assert that while college provides many valuable social, cultural, and recreational experiences for students, critical thinking ability and general reading and writing skills do not improve significantly. The failure to describe the connections between those social experiences and other kinds of learning is a key flaw in their work. The flaw may reflect the failure of the student affairs profession to document and articulate connections between pragmatist approaches to learning and the development of critical thinking skills. *Our Underachieving Colleges* by the former president of Harvard University, Derek Bok (2006), also addresses the issue of student learning from the perspective of transdisciplinary concerns, such as preparation for citizenship, building character, and living in a global society along with learning to think and communicate. He too finds current approaches to student learning seriously deficient.

The reasons student learning is such a problem have been discussed at length throughout this book. A simple but powerful way to frame this problem is the following: Teaching methods used in many college classrooms are not informed by recently developed knowledge about the ways people learn; student affairs activities help students learn, but they are not considered teaching. What we have here is the blind men and the elephant problem. The tools that could help enhance student learning are currently available, but different sets of tools are contained within historic, rigid borders. The methods that could be developed to enhance student learning, make it more powerful and transformative, are theoretically endless, but borders must be crossed, removed, or made permeable. Categories such as academic learning and academic credit must be reconsidered. Student affairs professionals must be able to explain what kind of learning occurs across the historic divide between the classroom and student life. We need new maps for this very new territory of learning through multiple modalities around common human concerns. This new map represents a constantly moving, incomprehensibly complex process in which the boundaries between teaching and learning, teaching and research, and teaching and managing are increasingly blurred into a process better described as a cycle of noticing, inquiring, acting, and evaluating. All members of a university community may participate, and all perspectives should receive respect. Agreement is not required, but understanding is a very worthwhile goal.

PART THREE

APPLICATIONS AND
IMPLICATIONS

The next part of this book contains descriptions of integrated programs that are designed to help students learn with their minds and hearts, learn to use data, and learn context and history. In keeping with the thesis of this book, that learning is an integrated process, the chapters describe institutional leadership and context, mentorship, service-learning, ethics education, intergroup dialogue, and first-year experience (FYE) programs.

Chapter 8 on leadership is written by Elsa M. Núñez, president of Eastern Connecticut State University. Núñez has been very successful in articulating goals for integrated learning and helping all segments of her staff work together to accomplish these goals with a student body that consists primarily of first-generation students.

Mentorship through Husky Sport, a program at the University of Connecticut that brings together Division 1 college athletes from privileged and underprivileged backgrounds with younger boys in the inner city of Hartford, one of the poorest cities in the country, is discussed in Chapter 9. The college athletes provide role models for the younger boys while they help them develop a sense of wider possibilities for their own future. Chapter author Vernon Percy, a former athlete, is program coordinator and mentor to the student athletes.

Julie Beth Elkins in Chapter 10 on service-learning discusses the complexity of finding one's own sense of purpose in life and exploring avenues that support learning processes that help bring purpose to fruition. The journey is described from the perspective of the service-learning coordinator and from the perspective of a student who is committed to service as civic engagement. Elkins is assistant dean of University College at Indiana University-Purdue University at Indianapolis.

Ethics must be learned intellectually and experientially if students are to have a functional sense of ethical decision making in life contexts. In Chapter 11 on transformative teaching and learning in a business class, Sarah Stookey addresses the issue of ethics education on campus and among a group of middle school students from low-income families who are learning to write simple business plans. Stookey is associate professor of business at Central Connecticut State University.

Intergroup dialogue, a program created at the University of Michigan, is designed to help people talk about significant personal and group differences in depth over an extended period of time. Chapter 12 author Craig John Alimo is a facilitator and a member of the research team that assesses program outcomes. The program is now in place on a wide range of campuses.

FYE courses are becoming a widespread phenomenon as part of a national effort to support student success in higher education, and there are many forms of FYE programs. The one described in Chapter 13 by Christopher Pudlinski and Scott Hazan focuses on processes that help create such programs across borders on a campus that is unionized in a manner that often makes collaboration between academic faculty and student affairs staff members difficult. Pudlinski is a professor of communications and director of the FYE program at Central Connecticut State University, and Hazan is director of student activities.

8

LEADERSHIP AND CONTEXT

The Central Role of Student Affairs at a Public Liberal Arts University

Elsa M. Núñez

When I arrived on the campus of Eastern Connecticut State University in May 2006 as Eastern's sixth president, I was excited about the possibilities. Having worked for many years at Ramapo College, the public liberal arts university of New Jersey, I felt very comfortable with Eastern's liberal arts mission. I was especially excited by the fact the university was ending its previous five-year strategic planning cycle, for that meant my first priority as president would be to facilitate a vision and a strategic plan for Eastern's future. It was an opportunity to lead cultural transformation and new academic and student life initiatives as we strived to become a premier liberal arts college.

I was confident about the faculty and staff's willingness to accept the challenge. I could see that the people at Eastern worked closely together as a team and were engaged in the local and state communities beyond the campus. I also was impressed with the innovation and creativity I found in faculty, students, and staff alike. It was my strong feeling the campus had the capacity to manage the changes the university was poised to make. Eastern in 2006 was ready to dramatically advance its mission as Connecticut's public liberal arts university. As the process of planning and implementing our vision has unfolded, this transformation has taken on a life of its own, and today has had an impact on every corner of our operations. This chapter focuses on the progress that has particularly occurred in the Division of Student Affairs.

The Planning Process

When we began our new strategic planning cycle in 2007, it was immediately clear that building a collaborative process that involved the entire campus would be the starting point and the key to our success in realizing a preferred future. It has been my experience that broad-based participation not only yields more ideas, but better, more mature ideas that have been developed collaboratively by teams of people based on a shared vision and shared values.

Faculty and staff eagerly accepted the task of working together to plan our next five years. In the end, more than 250 people, including alumni and members of our local community, participated in developing the 2008–2013 Strategic Plan, devoting more than 10,000 hours over a 14-month period to create a vision and a blueprint for our future. The process yielded 18 closely linked strategic initiatives with 63 separate benchmarks, all sharing a conceptual basis and a focus on the two key institutional measures of retention and graduation.

An initial planning phase featured four committees that looked at (a) demographic, economic, and other forces that would influence our future; (b) the ideas that govern our work—Eastern's mission, values, and vision; (c) strategies that could make the university distinctive on the regional and national stages; and (d) opportunities to better align our internal processes to create an effective, student-centered model of engaged learning. This last committee was cochaired by the vice president of student affairs and one academic dean, in recognition that a closer relationship between academic affairs and student affairs would be essential to our success. All four committees were cross-functional, bringing together representatives of academic affairs, student affairs, and other departments to build a model for our future success.

Following the work of these initial four planning groups, 18 strategic initiatives were developed by implementation teams, again composed of members from across the campus. Goals, objectives, activities, and assessment measures were the product of wide-ranging perspectives, as faculty, student affairs staff, and other personnel came together for a common purpose. In terms of student affairs involvement, several dozen student affairs staff participated in 15 of the 18 strategic initiative implementation teams.

The result has been an invigorating synergy on campus. Of course, such synergy is not accidental; it was intentional and planned. It has been rewarding to me to see how committed people from departments across the campus have been able to work more closely as they have implemented new systems to support student success academically and in student affairs functions throughout the campus.

A Model of Engaged Learning

Since Eastern was designated the public liberal arts university of Connecticut in 1998, Eastern's administrators have worked hard to better understand and articulate a preferred model of teaching and learning. Eastern's new model of engaged learning has been informed by a review of the work of such organizations as the National Survey of Student Engagement and the American Association of Colleges and Universities. The model envisions an integrated liberal arts experience that links all of a student's academic, social, and cocurricular activities into a cohesive whole. The academic program—first-year experiences, a liberal arts core, internships, undergraduate research, service-learning, cultural awareness and capstone experiences—is supported by many university departments. Community service, student employment, and even intramurals are all seen as necessary for the complete development of a student's intellectual, physical, and emotional well-being. In such an integrated model, every element of a student's day is tied together—classroom, residential, cocurricular—with a clear academic goal and a plan for achieving it in four years.

Many of the elements of this model of engaged learning existed in some form on Eastern's campus before we began our strategic planning process, but they were generally neither connected nor necessarily linked to a clear desired outcome.

The Changing Role of Student Affairs

Almost 100 years ago at schools such as Eastern in its earlier life as the Willimantic State Normal School, nonacademic staff were present to watch over their young students, providing protection, discipline, and out-of-class activities. In loco parentis was taken seriously. This was vividly evident on our own campus (ca. 1930), when even parents were not allowed into their daughters' dormitory rooms, and students were escorted from the residence hall to the library, a scant 20 yards across from the portico. The role of residential staff was limited to staffing the dormitories, without a canon of theory to guide their practice. There was no attempt to link academic life and student life, and the student activities that did take place were rarely intended as cocurricular opportunities.

Over the past 30 to 40 years, the concept of student affairs professionals as educators has emerged. *The Student Learning Imperative*, published by the American College Personnel Association (1996), encouraged more connections between student affairs and other university departments. In addition, student affairs department staff have worked to link more services in their areas. The growth in professionalism among student affairs officers has also been a function of new challenges—technology, multiculturalism, shifting demographics, equal opportunity, and the changing moral climate on campus. Even as student affairs functions became more centralized, and a greater emphasis was placed on a holistic student development model, functional separations in student affairs and academic affairs still existed. Today, at Eastern and in other institutions, the next step has been to see student affairs staff move from being support players to full partners in providing students with an integrated academic and student life experience that stimulates their intellectual, social, and personal development. By working side by side with academic affairs and other departments to plan and implement a common vision, student affairs at Eastern has truly come into its own. The Division of Student Affairs also has aligned its entire operations with learning outcomes developed by the Council for the Advancement of Standards in Higher Education (2010), which include intellectual growth, personal development, interpersonal skills, a commitment to humanitarian concerns, and practical competence. Division administrators have built their assessment plan to ensure these learning outcomes are met in all their programs.

Sequential and Cumulative

With national data showing that living on campus improves retention and graduation rates, connecting and integrating a student's academic and campus experience is a critical component of student success at a residential, undergraduate liberal arts college. In particular, cocurricular and residence hall activities and programs that augment and support a student's intellectual development clearly have been shown to improve retention and graduation rates (Kuh, Kinzie, Schuh, Whitt, & Associates, 2005).

The support provided by the Division of Student Affairs for Eastern's engaged learning model paralleled several key characteristics of the university's academic model: Since all student experiences on campus should reinforce each other, the teaching/learning plan must be *comprehensive* and *integrated*, and learning is *sequential* and *cumulative*, which means timing and conceptual relationships in the teaching and learning process are also critical. This concept of learning and development as a sequential process that results in advanced skills and knowledge makes perfect sense not only for our academic approach but also for the other systems Eastern has put into place to support a student's academic program. For instance, we have introduced a four-stage advising model as part of our campuswide Student Success Network. As it has been implemented, academic staff members, such as tutors and advisers, work seamlessly with student affairs staff, such as career services counselors and housing staff, to provide advising and counseling in formal settings as well as in the residence halls. Even before freshmen start their first semester at Eastern, a team of academic and student affairs staff members presents a summer orientation program that provides information on campus resources and services to help them make the transition to college.

Early Intervention Leads to Retention

Eastern's Six-Week Educational Enrichment Program (SWEEP) is perhaps the clearest example of the full partnership between student affairs and academic affairs staff in our retention efforts. The program is designed to assist all first-year residential students during the transition from high school to college in response to national data that indicates freshmen students are most at risk during their first six weeks. Keeping students on campus during the weekend, encouraging students to live on campus throughout their time at Eastern, integrating students quickly into campus life, and providing access to campus resources to improve college survival skills are all goals of the program. SWEEP events include hall and floor socials, dinners attended by resident assistants (RAs) and resident hall directors, roommate contracts, one-on-one conversations between RAs and individual students to build connections, and RA-initiated programs that focus on academics, life skills, and current events. In 2009–2010, 33 SWEEP events were attended by 2,600 students. One of the most beneficial programs during SWEEP, "A Major Decision," is a collaboration between the Offices of Academic Affairs, Academic Advisement, and Career Services to assist freshmen in selecting their academic major. Declaring a major early is another positive factor in improving retention and graduation rates.

Liberal Arts Work

A key element of the engaged learning model is the opportunity for skills application that experiential learning provides our students. At Eastern we have established a graduation requirement ("Liberal Arts Work!") to ensure that all students will have at least one preprofessional experience before graduation. Four main categories of experiential learning—internships, undergraduate research/creative expression, paid co-ops, and service-learning courses—can fulfill the graduation requirement. The leadership for implementing this initiative has again come from our academic and student affairs units, from key faculty leaders, as well as from members of our community service and career services staffs in the Division of Student Affairs.

Using the U.S. Department of Education's Title III grants program and Nellie Mae Education Foundation grants, an associate director and career counselor were hired to provide career counseling to students earlier in their Eastern career. The Office of Career Services also assists students in identifying internship and paid co-op opportunities that best match their majors and career interests, provides faculty with support in connecting academic programs to short- and long-term internship sites, and serves as liaison to those internships and co-ops. Of special note is the work being done to bring career development services to freshman students in the form of faculty workshops, classroom presentations, and residence hall programming.

Service to the Community

Another area where we have seen transformation taking place on campus has been in community engagement. When I arrived on campus, residential students had to commit to eight hours of community service annually. While the volume of work performed was impressive, there was no attempt to link this community service to classroom learning, no attempt to match student energy and time to community priorities, and no attempt to create a campuswide culture of service. The Office of Housing and Residential Life was left alone to manage the process.

In our current model, everyone participates in service, reinforcing our university core value of social responsibility. While the Center for Community Engagement (CCE) was established in fall 2009 to support service-learning courses and coordinate community service, student clubs also organize and conduct service projects, as does our housing office. Many of the events and programs bring all these organizations together, including, for example, spring cleanups for local towns.

More faculty are connecting classroom learning to opportunities to serve the community, with the CCE providing support by linking faculty with community clients. What was once a mandated activity limited to the housing office has now become a campuswide commitment to serving the community while linking service-learning to our students' overall liberal arts experiences. And *community* has grown to include everything from tutoring middle school children in Willimantic, our hometown, to building Habitat for Humanity homes in West Virginia and installing wind turbines at schools in Jamaica.

Club Participation

Aligning club activities with academic programming while also emphasizing increased participation has been another key initiative in our student affairs plan, further reinforcing our engaged learning model. Reflecting this collaborative model, many clubs are coadvised by faculty and student affairs staff.

Eastern's experience demonstrates that participation in cocurricular clubs, rather than weighing down a student's schedule, actually improves academic performance. The average grade point average of students who participate in clubs is 3.05, compared to an average of 2.88 for all full-time students. Club leaders do even better at 3.13. In the past four years, the number of clubs has increased 40%, the number of students participating in clubs has increased by 66%, and the number of club events is up 40%. A Dean's Cup competition also has been instituted where the students in our 12 residence halls compete for the cup based on participation in academic, social, and cultural programming, as well as community service. Now in its fourth year, the program gives each hall an opportunity to display hall and school spirit while promoting the personal, social, and academic development of each participating student.

The renovation and expansion of our student center in fall 2007 also has been a key to bringing all student clubs under one roof and allowed us to dramatically expand student activities programming. This includes activities on the weekend, which keep students on campus and helps to increase retention and graduation rates.

In addition to services aimed at serving the entire campus, we have also improved and expanded services to women, minorities, veterans, and the lesbian, gay, bisexual, transgender, queer, and questioning community. Inclusion is one of our core values, and we work hard to ensure that all members of the campus community are respected, protected, and supported.

Stewardship, Sustainability, and Energy Conservation

Eastern is recognized as a leader in Green Campus initiatives in New England, and was named one of the nation's Green Colleges by the *Princeton Review* in 2010. This commitment to a sustainable future can be seen in academic programs such as the major in sustainable energy studies, the U.S. Green Building Council's certification of a number of buildings on campus, and the statewide outreach conducted by Eastern's Institute for Sustainable Energy. Again, the Division of Student Affairs is actively involved, supporting a student-led recycling program in the residence halls, encouraging student clubs to conduct campuswide environmental awareness programs, and conducting community beautification programs through the CCE.

Conclusion

The transformation I have described is hardly over. It is an ongoing process, and we realize that our long-term success will depend on continuing to bring new perspectives to campus. Understanding and supporting our expanded vision will be a fundamental skill set for new faculty and staff hires in the future. College students who are just now bearing the fruits of the new model of integrated engaged learning will become the student affairs professionals and institutional leaders of tomorrow. As we receive feedback from students and alumni, I suspect that our model will undergo additional changes over time.

Clearly, however, we are on the right path. If the immediate measure of our success is graduating our students on time, and the preferred model of engaged learning brings the entire campus experience—in and out of class—into focus, then the process of integrating our academic and student affairs systems into a larger whole is successful. Our students are emerging from their Eastern experience as mature adults, serious scholars, and engaged citizens. And our campus community of faculty and staff members has never been more unified in its purpose and its daily enterprise.

Student affairs professionals have been part of this transformation from the earliest stages of the planning process. The examples cited in this chapter demonstrate a planned approach to student development in the Division of Student Affairs, as well as opportunities to link with academic affairs and other staff across the campus. Less than a year ago, *U.S. News and World Report* ranked Eastern as the 28th regional university in the North, the first time we have ever been in its tier one rankings. We take this as a sign of progress and the motivation to continue finding ways to better integrate and strengthen the student experience on the Eastern Connecticut State University campus.

References

American College Personnel Association. (1996). *The student learning imperative.* Washington, DC: Author.

Council for the Advancement of Standards in Higher Education. (2010). *CAS professional standards for higher education* (7th ed.) Washington, DC: Author.

Kuh, G., Kinzie, J., Schuh, E., Whitt, E., & Associates. (2005). *Student success in college: Creating conditions that matter.* San Francisco, CA: Jossey-Bass.

9

CREATING INTEGRATED SELVES

Sport and Service-Learning

Vernon Percy

O n Tuesdays and Thursdays during the academic year student athletes travel by van from the rural surroundings of the University of Connecticut to inner-city Hartford to mentor youths who are involved in a sport-based after-school program. The student athletes are a mixture of current and former service-learning classmates from diverse backgrounds. It is a warm April day. No longer are the college students focused on the newly revamped neighborhood recreational center where the program occurs, but rather they are preparing to meet with youngsters awaiting their guidance. However, months earlier it was evident this once dilapidated space was quite unlike what many of these individuals had experienced during their student/athlete careers at the university or during their youth sport experience. The remaining student athletes understood the meaning of the lack of facilities and resources, which was a "make do with what you've got" sentiment. For all involved, the encounter proved to be the beginning of an emerging awareness of the sport-related barriers facing youngsters in urban environments as well as the advantages enjoyed by the student athletes from more privileged environments. Moreover, through the student athlete's relationship with the after-school program community, as well as their service-learning course, some began to reconsider their sense of self and purpose.

Student Athlete Context—The Promise

To understand the significance of what student athletes learned as a result of the program it is important to provide an understanding of the role of the college athletic experience on their development. As adolescents and young adults we tend to understand the world as offering a realm of possibilities. However, we find ourselves limited by roles and identities we accept without criticism, allowing the ways others define such roles to influence the meaning we give to ourselves. Sport culture often creates expectations through promises about what possibilities exist for young adults in college. Often these promises involve athletic participation, an academic degree, and the potential for a good job afterward. How realistic are these promises for collegiate athletes?

A great majority of student athletes, particularly in Division I, attend college with high hopes of experiencing success in the form of fame and glory, opportunities to play professionally, and to obtain a degree. For many the idea of playing professionally fades quickly as these young men and women realize they are no longer the big fish in a little pond. From the beginning, often prior to attending college, student athletes pursue sport as a career, engaging in the role as a major part of their identity. A deeper exploration of the question "who am I" is not always encouraged by their network of family, friends, coaches, and community. This essential aspect of becoming a young adult, self-exploration, is often given only cursory attention if not absolutely neglected.

A common pitch for athletic coaches seeking to sign recruits is the promise of athletic participation at a high level, the use of top-rated facilities to hone their athletic skills and acumen, the possibility of athletic success and even championships, a top-rated education, as well as the possibility of a career in whatever area they are interested. I've heard coaches lend credence to the emphasis on getting a solid degree by claiming that the particular sport program, athletic department, and university have provided these young men and women every opportunity to eliminate any excuses for failure. Have they? Despite the pitch, I believe that for some programs, a sincere effort to develop young adults comes with a cost to their sense of self and identity. I agree with Parks (2000), who stated:

> The central work of the young adult era in the cycle of human life is not
> located in any of these tasks or circumstances per se. Rather, the *promise*

and vulnerability of young adulthood lie in the experience of the birth of critical awareness and the dissolution and recomposition of the meaning of self, other world, and "God." (p. 8)

If one were to inquire more closely about the expectations of university officials for their athletes, as well as the opportunities provided for young adults to dwell in faith, what would one find? It is no secret that collegiate sport, particularly Division I-A revenue-producing athletics, has been severely criticized for low graduation and retention rates of its athletes, especially African Americans in football and basketball (Percy, 2007). Many of these athletes never receive their degrees in the four or five years promised and never fully explore, pursue, or obtain the degrees and enter into the careers that might have been most suitable for them. What of the student athletes who have not been provided opportunities to examine more deeply their sense of self? Parks (2000) goes on to state, "Within a distracted, indifferent, or exploiting culture, however, young adulthood may be squandered on dreams too small to match the potential of the young adult soul, or it simply may be cast adrift in the unexamined currents of mere circumstance" (p. 8).

Community Service as a Pedagogical Tool

I conducted interviews with African American student athletes who graduated from college and participated in a Division I revenue-producing sport at major universities (Percy, 2007). For each young adult, giving back to his community was highly important. In fact it was, on some level, a motivating factor for each of the five young men even prior to college and became even more important as they proceeded. Each individual subscribed to the idea that the community helped him, and he wanted to "raise up" those who may not have had opportunities, who may be in similar predicaments as these young men were when they were young. They all recounted close mentoring relationships in which someone else supported, challenged, and inspired them. While each of these young men participated in community-service efforts structured by their football or basketball program or the athletics department, they did not express a truer understanding of themselves with relation to the experience other than its being charitable in some way.

It became evident these men were interested in moving beyond their surface understanding to a deeper examination of their phenomenological assumptions.

How Learning Is Organized

The after-school sport-based program for boys is part of a larger community network/partnership that collaborates to promote healthier physical and psychosocial development for inner-city youths. As part of this program, a service-learning component exists to engage undergraduates in this effort. The network also includes graduate students, faculty, community families, professionals, local school networks, and after-school agencies, among others. Included in the undergraduate enrollment are regular students from various majors and backgrounds as well as the student athletes. Because of the time demands placed on student athletes to attend classes, practice, train, travel, and so forth, student athlete involvement is usually limited to the off season (and to juniors and seniors who may have more time to get away). For example, members of the football team would enroll in the spring and complete their hours prior to spring football training. Because the after-school program occurs throughout the academic year, essentially four to five days a week, student athletes are able to avoid typical accessibility and time barriers that cause them to miss out on many other campus activities or initiatives. The service-learning course is taught by a faculty member or a doctoral student and is intentionally designed to offer student athletes opportunities to reflect upon themselves in a way that is associated with being a student athlete, for example, what is the meaning of athletic participation in their own lives, and what are their hopes for the future?

Student athlete involvement transcends the usual role of being an athlete on campus. Although youngsters in the community view them as athletic role models, they begin to know the college students on a deeper level. The student athletes develop relationships with the children and with the community. They begin to understand many of the sociopolitical forces that shape the lives of boys within the community. This exposure prompts students to consider what Parks (2000) described as some of the Big Enough Questions, such as: "Why is suffering so pervasive? What constitutes meaningful work? What are the values and limitations of my culture? What do I want the future to look like—for me, others, and the world?" (p. 137).

Student athletes are not simply receiving credit for attending a service-learning lecture. They are also engaged in a learning community focused on addressing larger social problems, and in doing so encounter real-life issues that prompt self-exploration of the meaning and purpose of their lives, and they begin to consider the lives they have.

In contrast, student athletes also attend courses in which they are distant participants as are so many of their nonathlete peers. They sit in courses that reify knowledge through dull lectures, not understanding the relevance of abstract constructions to their own lives and futures. Experiences in the service-learning course and the university's Husky Sport community outreach program allow student athletes to reflect upon themselves and relate this understanding to other courses such as sociology, philosophy, and political science. The Husky Sport initiative, which pairs university students with local schoolchildren, was developed by sport management faculty but also includes faculty in nutrition, athletic training, and counseling. While student athletes from a variety of majors are encouraged to be a part of the service-learning experience, student athletes in sport management are enrolled in other courses that use Husky Sport programming to better understand concepts related to those courses. Husky Sport is an organic and coherent systematic culture in an otherwise inorganic and incoherent culture. More work needs to be done to change the larger culture so that its focus has more meaning and purpose and is systematic in nature.

Mentoring

A critical ingredient to the success of the Husky Sport program is the mentoring relationship between the student athletes and the youngsters involved in the program. While sport is a common lure that prompts participation on behalf of both groups, it is their relationship that is key to the successful personal development of children and college students alike. This relationship-based model, as understood from a college student development perspective, is also a motivating factor resulting in a focus on establishing healthy mentoring roles between faculty and undergraduates and graduate students. These relationships should become a platform that gives students the space to reflect on what Parks (2000) referred to as "questions of meaning, purpose, and faith" (p. 138). For student athletes such exploration allows them to acknowledge the value of their role as athletes (specifically, as athletic role models to young boys) and to transcend their athletic identity by questioning its meaning and purpose.

Networking

As with the youngsters in the Husky Sport boys program, student athletes are encouraged to be active participants in the decision making of the Husky Sport program—every voice is welcome. Getting the boys to trust us and feel as if they belong is a major effort for all adults involved. Much of the literature on student athletes maintains that they suffer from isolation from the rest of the campus community. This Husky Sport program provides student athletes with an opportunity to broaden their understanding of their communities, not simply the student athlete community or the university community, and create new quality relationships.

Why Does All This Matter?

An argument can be made that while student athletes are one of the most visible populations on campus, they are also invisible and misunderstood. Being as isolated as they are physically and psychologically, it is incumbent upon universities to intentionally design opportunities that are accessible to student athletes that allow them to create a new sense of meaning for themselves and the world. Doing so will enhance the role of student athletes by transcending the preconceived notions they have about themselves. The implications can potentially be transformative in how student athletes understand their lives.

While community service opportunities are available to student athletes through the athletic department or team-related relationships, much of these services are what I would call in and out. I am certain these experiences are useful for student athletes and for the individuals and communities being served—but is it transformative? What is the current organization and structure of universities, athletic departments, and programs? Do they encourage transformational learning? What opportunities for transformational learning can be provided?

References

Parks, S. D. (2000). *Big questions, worthy dreams: Mentoring young adults in their search for meaning.* San Francisco, CA: Jossey-Bass.

Percy, V. E. (2007). *Understanding identity and psychosocial functioning through the lived experiences of African American collegiate athletes participating in revenue-producing sports: A hermeneutic phenomenological approach.* Unpublished doctoral dissertation, University of Connecticut (Dissertation collection, AAI13293721).

10

ENGAGED LEARNING

Beyond the Ivory Tower

Julie Beth Elkins

As far as I am concerned, learning through experience is the best way to learn. Theory is all well and good, but I'd rather go observe rivers than sit in a windowless lecture hall and talk about them.

—Shannon, engaged college student

Education for human development is the creation of a human learning environment within which individuals, teachers, and social systems interact and utilize developmental tasks for personal growth and social betterment.

(Crookston, 1975, p. 57)

History spins a tale of higher education founded in the spirit of developing young adults to become civic leaders so they may work to advance communities and the nation (Astin, 1996; Dewey, 1916; Eyler & Giles, 1999). The ability to evoke learning from real-life situations changes the entire dynamic of learning. Not only does it allow students to create meaning from information, it also attaches the heart to the head as people reflect on their unique experiences in the context of their individual lives. Engaged learning, described in this text as integrated or transformative learning, closely mirrors the natural learning process as described by Zull (2006). Natural engaged learning always involves gathering, reflecting upon, creating, and testing new knowledge and insights. Unfortunately, this approach to learning, which dramatically changes our understanding of teaching, contradicts the traditional learning paradigms typically used in higher education. Engaged learning integrates heart, mind, behavior, and meaning, while traditional learning emphasizes mind almost to the exclusion of the other three elements of learning. Engaged learning assumes emotional involvement, testing of old ideas, and construction of new ideas.

Civic engagement is one of the more popular forms of experiential engaged learning on campuses today (Astin et al., 2006; Bringle & Hatcher, 1996). It suggests "an active collaboration that builds on the resources, skills, expertise, and knowledge of the campus and community to improve the quality of life in communities in a manner that is consistent with the campus mission" (Indiana University-Purdue University Indiana [IUPUI] Task Force on Civic Engagement, 2004). Portland State University elevates civic engagement as the focus of its mission, "Let Knowledge Serve the City," and proclaims that "Oregon Is Our Classroom." Engaged learning breaks down the wall between classroom learning and the creation of personal meaning. Engagement goes beyond service; it exemplifies the reality of mutual influence and responsibility among all community members. Engagement improves the quality of life for the community and for the engaged student. Civic engagement uses knowledge, skills, time, talents, and finances from all participants and applies them to community problems. It must be reciprocal so that both parties, the student and the community, profit from the engagement. Civic engagement as a teaching/learning modality demonstrates that the information transmission, or fact recall approach to teaching/learning, is obsolete and potentially destructive.

For civic engagement to provoke learning, facilitators from academic affairs and student affairs must overcome the cognition/affect split that defines so much of our work in the academic community. This process is structurally difficult and intellectually confusing because it shifts the dominant faculty paradigm of learning from cognition to a cognitive/experiential cycle that engages rather than excludes emotions. For student affairs professionals, engaged learning benefits dramatically from the infusion of academic content as part of the reflection process. However, student affairs professionals often do not believe they are academically competent to deliver or discuss academic content, despite their skill in facilitating discussions about personal meaning and emotional responses to experience. Florida State University provides a notable exception to this historical divide with its Center for

Leadership and Civic Engagement, which is codesigned and cofacilitated by academicians and student affairs professionals. The work of the center is grounded in a theory to practice model that includes Heifetz's (1994) work on adaptive leadership, Kouzes and Posner's (2008) work on exemplary practices of leadership, and Wheatley's (2007) work on chaos, change, and community organizing. In addition, foundational work in student development and pedagogy, including *Learning Reconsidered* (Keeling, 2004); the leadership identity development model by Komives, Longerbeam, Mainella, and Osteen (2005); and Kolb's (1984) experiential learning cycle, are also part of the theoretical framework of the center. The curriculum includes critical thinking, relationship building, group dynamics, the dynamics of intergroup partnerships, and the study of social and economic systems. Student learning goals are based on demonstration of learning in these areas, and the curriculum is organized developmentally. All learning has an experiential component. The staff of the center includes faculty members, student affairs staff members, and students (see http://thecenter.fsu.edu/).

Civic engagement involves learning about self, community, and the wider world. Excluding any of these elements undermines the power and value of the learning experience. Civic engagement involves acquisition of skills, expansion of knowledge, and awareness of the broader scope of human activity. It is a developmental process on all levels. The model of civic engagement in the next section provides a view of student progress along a continuum from simple involvement to change agentry. This chapter examines several key components of civic engagement illustrated by the specific experiences of one engaged college student. It addresses early patterns of learning, theoretical foundations, the power of reflection, the fear of political power, and difficulties developing a reliable assessment measure for success.

Continuum of Engagement

Civic engagement entails a slow escalation of increased involvement, deliberate planning, constant nurturing, trust building, honest intentionality, reciprocal exchange, and sincere commitment. It is not built overnight. The continuum of engagement model (Elkins & Morrow, 2010) demonstrates a progressive, sequential framework to describe the development of engaged relationships between students and communities. The time frame for this process is fluid, but the sequence seems to be progressive and linear.

Most students begin with some form of simple involvement: attending an event or advancing individual learning beyond classroom requirements about a specific topic, language, or interest. Students must take an interest in the subject beyond their academic assignments. Even though the movement can be quite small, it requires some low-level engagement to begin. There must be some evidence of the student's personal concern about the issue. The next phase, interaction, requires a level of interchange or relationship, such as a student joining a student group or organization. Others may further their commitment to an interest by purchasing some type of athletic equipment to participate in a particular sport or by wearing clothing associated with a specific group, providing some form of interconnection between an individual and others. An example of some advanced forms of interaction is participating in the Martin Luther King Day of Service or in other one-time volunteer days.

Investment, the next phase, signals advanced commitment not only to the interest area but to a group situated in the larger system of the institution. There are usually many experiences to choose from. The mission of the group may be narrow or broad. Some leaders, such as a student body president or student trustee, are elected and make final decisions involving large amounts of money or exert significant influence on the university. Other students may have more individual experiences, such as participating in an alternative to spring break or a study abroad program. Individuals have high levels of experiential learning and interactions beyond the university but may not develop a long-term commitment to an organization.

Students who are involved in civic engagement demonstrate some type of "active collaboration with the community that builds on the resources, skills, expertise, and knowledge of the campus and community to improve the quality of life" (IUPUI, 2002). For example, students not only vote but would also provide leadership for increasing voter registration. They might actively serve in a community-campus partnership, conduct community-based research, or gather oral histories from community members.

Change agents are students who are actively engaged in influencing policy, laws, and practices on campus, the larger community, and even globally. One example is active involvement in a public interest research group that has been influential in passing bills to increase bottle recycling and container-deposit legislation, thus influencing changes in production methods and policies used by large corporate soda companies. Another example is the Faces of Student Aid, a Facebook campaign that lobbies for increased access to higher education, targeting Pell Grants and the Supplemental Education Opportunity Grant program. It has mobilized students across the nation to communicate directly with U.S. senators to increase access to higher education. Some students in specific groups rise to leadership positions and become change agents. For instance, all members of an undergraduate student government may unanimously support legislation on increased access to higher education, which demonstrates investment. However, one or two students may emerge as change agents by attending a retreat on how to lobby Congress and then organizing a bus trip to Washington, D.C., to testify before the Senate on the importance of access to higher education.

The framework in figure 10.1 illustrates a student's journey along the continuum of engagement. The student who was chosen as the case study for this chapter has sought out a progression of deepening engagement opportunities along the continuum through her high school and college careers.

FIGURE 10.1
Continuum of Engagement

Involvement ➡ Interaction ➡ Investment ➡ Civic Engagement ➡ Change Agent

Shannon is a second-generation college student who grew up in a small rural university town in New England. The family is White. She is 19 years old, majoring in environmental science and minoring in French. Her family was actively engaged with the community and the world. They participated in a religious community, voted in every election, and were involved with town politics and community service. They listened to and discussed broadcasts on National Public Radio as a family and valued engagement and service. Many students have familial experiences similar to Shannon's, participating with their parents from an early age. There is evidence that family and religious organizations are key factors of influence that teach children and young adults about civic engagement (McIntosh, Hart, & Youniss, 1977). It is important to note that "socialization scholars have provided evidence that civic training in adolescence can influence adult behavior" (Andolina, Jenkins, Zukin, & Keeter, 2003, p. 278). Shannon began volunteering with her family at the Maritime Museum at an early age. Her pattern of involvement in her K–12 experience led to her connections with several clubs and organizations within her first month of attending college full-time.

Interacting With the World

Involvement is the gateway to civic engagement. A major theoretician in the domain of student involvement and its effects on transformative learning, Alexander Astin has devoted much of his life's work to demonstrating the importance of students' being involved and interacting in the college environment. There is significant evidence that service-learning is a positive vehicle of engagement for college students (Astin, Antonino, Cress, & Astin, 1996). Engagement studies (Astin & Sax, 1998) have revealed the relationship between academic achievement and the positive influences of place of residence (living on campus), participating in honors programs, and student group involvement. Quality interactions are more than a stepping-stone to civic engagement. There is also strong evidence they are predictors of academic success in measurable terms such as grades, retention, and graduation rates (Cress, Burack, Giles, Elkins, & Stevens 2010; Vogelgesang & Astin, 2000). Interaction provides advanced opportunities for building skills in areas that count the most, learning to work with others, learning about difference, and developing effective communication skills and an increased understanding of self.

Leading the Way for Others

As a high school student, Shannon started a fencing club. She had been fencing in the community but saw an opportunity to compete for the school. She wanted to share her love of fencing with her classmates. She fused her intellectual, physical, and manual skills and interpersonal competence to create a large outlet for herself and her peers while in high school (Chickering & Reisser, 1993). Shannon added another dimension to her own identity when she sought out her first study abroad experience in her sophomore year. She said that she was bored learning in a classroom, but was convinced that foreign language is useful. Going abroad was her way of reigniting her own learning. Shannon negotiated new languages, traditions, norms, and foods, and discovered the art of shaping and leading her own learning beyond the classroom. Shannon was able to study abroad twice as a high school student, which prepared her to seek out a semester-long experience abroad to learn about how another culture is advancing in her field of study. These heightened forms of engagement prepared her for new opportunities in the future and placed her in situations where her academic and personal learning fused into transformative experiences that motivated her to continue this journey with enthusiasm.

Civic Engagement

Student affairs professionals have often been hesitant to commit to civic engagement even though important gateway experiences, such as chaperoning spring break trips to impoverished areas or participating in local efforts with community groups such as Habitat for Humanity, have been available to them and their students. Perhaps the profession has been paralyzed by the political implications of fostering engaged citizenship since this is a more controversial process than simply teaching leadership skills for use in student organizations. Historically, a large majority of colleges and universities include principles of civic leadership in their mission statements, but leadership education seems to be restricted to campus activities (Rudolph, 1991). Faculty members are often engaged in the management of their own academic communities through involvement in university governance, although they tend not to connect this aspect of their work with teaching students. Student affairs professionals have far less opportunity to engage in campus governance because they are generally administrative employees, embedded in bureaucratic structures with no right to academic freedom of speech. "The first step in rebuilding civic life outside the academy is to rebuild civic life with the academy," according to Zelda Gamson (2000), a highly respected scholar in learning and organization of universities. This process will inevitably involve restructuring governance and conflict between current and emerging power structures. There is a built-in disconnect in the learning process when students are encouraged to become involved with significant civic issues off campus and are required to submit to either academic or student affairs authorities "for their own good" when they are in school. One might wonder what this bit of cognitive dissonance does to the learning process and the creation of community on campus.

Often we struggle to measure levels of civic engagement and resort to quantitative measures such as counting percentages of undergraduate voter registration and volunteer hours. Putnam (2000) has offered components of a comprehensive social capital index that assesses social capital in America by looking at measurements of community organization life, engagement in public affairs, volunteerism, informal sociability, and social trust. However, these instruments often fail to be connected to institutional missions, faculty reward systems, pedagogy, policies, and practices, and are therefore irrelevant to motivational factors for faculty members, student affairs professionals, or students.

For Shannon, civic engagement materialized in the form of an opportunity to participate in an honors summer internship program. "I accepted my internship because I had always wanted the combination of photography and science that it presented to me. That sort of interdisciplinary experience is what I really want," she said. Shannon was also attracted to the opportunity because she could have direct involvement with a community outside the university that was in need of research and the services she could provide as an intern. Shannon lived in the desert for several months during the summer, photographing sites for the community archives. An unexpected outcome of this experience was bonding with the site supervisor who became her mentor. "My mentor, Peter, showed me that it may be hard to pave the way to what one wants to do, but it can be done." The lesson far exceeded the goals of any program. Shannon learned she had the capacity to effect change and she could prevail over difficulties. This type of civic engagement ventures far beyond that of a day of service or the confines of a structured classroom. It provides an opportunity to live, work, and conduct research for a community. This is a true example of civic engagement where insight, reciprocal learning, and service happens for the student and the community. A question that arises in this context is about the skill level of the faculty mentor and whether Peter's willingness to involve himself personally and professionally with his student reflected a set of skills that is widespread among his colleagues. Engaged learning is a powerful pedagogical tool that requires skills most faculty members have not had the opportunity to develop. What potential roles might student affairs professionals play in helping these professors acquire and use both the skills and the knowledge of developmental psychology and ethics so engaged pedagogy could become more widespread?

Change Agent

Shannon's journey represents a fluid progression of experiences that prepared her for intentional actions as a change agent. While her early study abroad adventures were open and exploratory, as a college junior she chose a concentrated five-month institute to study sustainability in another country. Her intention was to expand her education so she could launch strategic action on her own campus and nationally. Like Shannon, change agents often have some type of internalized Otherness or eccentric nature linked to their identity. This may be a core identity such as race or sexual orientation or a chosen passion such as Shannon's favorite sport of fencing. This sense of Otherness provokes an awareness of different perspectives on problems since the student intuitively realizes his or her perspective on a particular issue may not be widely shared. Shannon also has demonstrated an action-oriented major, environmental science, with a strong commitment to creating change through sustainability.

> Most of the qualities in students that drive activism—increased sensitivity to social problems, motivation to address these problems, sophistication about effective strategies, and clarity about one's own values—are all essential to exercising responsible citizenship in a pluralistic democracy. They are also important education outcomes. (Chickering, 1998)

Broader Implications of Change Agentry for Learning and Engagement

> Is student activism on campus part of the civic agenda? If the answer is no, then a significant proportion of student leadership is excluded. This leadership will, rightly, believe that "civic" is a way of domesticating students' impulses for social justice, a way of channeling them into "nice" volunteer and service activities. (Chickering & Gamson, 1999; Gamson, 2000)

Fostering strong autonomy, critical thinking, questioning the status quo, organizing opportunities for community dialogue are just a few of the most precious outcomes of civic engagement. In one program, students at Providence College in Rhode Island are trained in deliberative dialogue. These students then teach high school students how to lead conversations about important school issues in formal and informal settings such as classrooms, homerooms, and lunchrooms. The high school students learn how to address issues of governance and policy in their own school and how to intervene effectively to influence change. The college students learn teaching and research skills, and the high school students learn how to interact with their own community in meaningful ways. Inevitably this process may provoke activism and possibly become disruptive. But it can and often does provide different perspectives on problem solving and makes alienation from learning far less pervasive at the high school and college levels.

It has been difficult for the members of the academy to recognize that student activism is on the rise because it looks different from the activism of the 1960s and 1970s. Students have embraced the power of social media and used the ability to launch coordinated, funded, strategic protests simultaneously across the country with the stroke of a text message. One of the most profound examples of this student mobilization for change has been in the arena of sweatshop labor and collegiate logowear. Thousands of students across the country have come together to form an organization called United Students Against Sweatshops (USAS), a profound example of engaged learning and civic engagement. In 1997 a college student had a summer internship placement with the Union of Needletrades, Industrial, and Textile Employees that spawned the idea to create a grass-roots national student-run organization. USAS now has over 250 college and university chapters with thousands of members who founded the independent monitoring organization Worker Rights Consortium with 180 college and university affiliates, and launched the groundbreaking campaign to change the enforcement of university codes of conduct to protect the rights of workers who sew for university logo apparel.

Change agents are now advancing second-order societal change, a fundamental break with the past that is a dramatic departure from current practice. New knowledge and new skills are needed to successfully implement second-order change, an innovative systemic change, a paradigm shift, and transformational change. The irony of this process, which seems to be increasing in intensity and speed as of this writing, is that nobody is teaching students how to do this work. They are learning from each other though "meet ups" and other forms of communication made possible by social media. Students are highly involved, providing leadership for change, engaging local and global communities, and addressing their problems from the Middle East to Wall Street; they have become civic leaders, change agents, and champions for democracy and justice around the world. They did not learn these skills in college, and they will not receive academic credit for their work. We must begin to ask ourselves what kinds of pedagogies support the education of students so they learn to care enough about the welfare of humanity to give their time and their knowledge to leadership for social benefit? What skills do members of the student affairs profession have that can contribute to helping faculty learn about engaged pedagogy? Student affairs professionals are already helping students learn about organization, decision making, leadership, conflict management, and marketing ideas and events. How can we use what we are already doing to support students who are willing to spend weeks sleeping outside on Wall Street to protest capitalist greed, or organizing American students so they refuse to buy college sports clothing made in sweatshops, or volunteering in inner-city schools to help our most vulnerable children learn to read, or volunteering at the local food bank while asking why in the richest country in the world are so many poor?

Reflections

Reflection is critical to this learning/action process, yet so many times it is not integrated into experiential learning. Traditional methods of reflection are facilitated in credit-bearing experiences and often require some type of integrated writing in the form of papers, testing, or projects. This kind of reflection can also occur in small seminars facilitated by staff members with appropriate group skills. Reflection often provokes disorientation and questioning of long-held values. Once again, most academic faculty members do not have the training to facilitate these kinds of group discussions, but many student affairs staff members do. We should be asking ourselves how much more powerful and transformative reflection processes might become if cofacilitated by student affairs professionals who have group and individual counseling skills in their repertoire. Anyone who had been involved in helping a White student understand privilege as a social construct knows how disorienting these insights often become. If a mentor is present to help students rethink their values, consider their place in the societal matrix, and consider responses to their new insights, students would be more likely to move through the shipwreck process (Parks, 2000) toward constructive resolutions.

Advanced integrated learning models often use senior projects, portfolios, or a capstone course to facilitate reflection to attach meaning to learning. The University of Michigan's Integrative Learning and MPortfolio initiative is specifically designed to help students integrate what they have learned in college as part of what is called the life-wide curriculum (Peet, 2011). Faculty members are taught about the organic nature of learning and then trained in the facilitation of interdisciplinary projects and student conversations. At Portland State University all students complete capstone projects designed to help them master advanced knowledge and skills in an interdisciplinary area. These courses are designed across the curriculum by the faculty to build cooperative learning communities by taking students out of the classroom and into the field. In these courses service-learning becomes more than a pedagogical framework. It enhances student learning while cultivating crucial life skills and abilities that are important both academically and professionally.

Despite the vast number of experiential learning and community-based experiences, Shannon had few reflective experiences integrated into her formal learning until she created one for herself. As a means of connection when living out of state on her own she started to document her experiences on Facebook to keep in touch with her friends and family. Not only did she write about her various culinary adventures cohabitating with a group of students who were all vegetarian (she previously had not been), she began to process her experiences, the interactions she had in the town, photographing in the desert, how it felt to be somewhere different, and how it felt to learn new things. She even began to write about the reciprocal relationship with the members of the community in contributing through research, and what she was learning about the people of the community. All this mental processing contributed to Shannon's ability to make meaning of her experiences and apply them to other aspects of her life (Baxter Magolda, 1999). The deficit in Shannon's formal learning process points out an important role for student affairs professionals in experiential learning. All experiential learning, including service-learning, raises the question, "What does all this mean to me and the people I care about?" That is a question student affairs professionals are skilled in helping students address. This process points out a key location for integrating academic and personal learning and suggests that experts in both aspects of the process should be involved in helping students explore these issues.

The value of being able to be conscious of our experiences and process them in an organized manner expressed through art (writing, music, drawing, painting, sculpting, and so on) is essential to enhancing the connection between new knowledge and the emotive component of the experience (the

head with the heart). Reflection is critical in helping people realize the connections between themselves and others, and themselves and the world
around them. It is quite amazing that Shannon stumbled upon the important outlet for advanced learning in a need to stay connected to her family
and friends. Shannon commented that her Facebook postings were one of
her most powerful learning experiences. It is also a living document in the
sense that she can revisit it and share it with others as time goes on, a way of
continuing the learning long past the actual experience.

Integrated learning opens up opportunities for a myriad of experiences
for the head and the heart. The gift of being able to work with students and
learn from their unique growing processes as they become civically engaged
in the world is a tremendous experience. I have watched students create new
university policies; actively serve on community-campus partnerships;
change town ordinances; run for state office; lobby for changes in state,
national, and global laws; question global business practices; begin national
dialogues; create national organizations; and develop new strategies to eliminate homelessness, hunger, sweatshop labor, racism, homophobia, and the
criminalization of marijuana. Students are becoming actively engaged by
leading and directing their own learning. "Civic learning enables people to
practice civic politics, or self-directed public action" (Boyte, 2008).

Perhaps Shannon said it best when she told me, "Being engaged showed
me that I can find a way to do whatever I want."

References

Andolina, M., Jenkins, K., Zukin, C., & Keeter, S. (2003). Habits from home, lessons from school: Influences on youth civic engagement. *American Political Science Association, 36*(2), 278–280.

Astin, A. (1996). Involvement in learning revisited: Lessons we have learned. *Journal
of College Student Development, 37*(2), 123–133.

Astin, A. W., & Sax, L. J. (1998). How undergraduates are affected by service participation. *Journal of College Student Development, 39*(3), 123–133.

Astin, A. W., Vogelgesang, L. J., et al. (2006). *Understanding the effects of service-
learning: A study of students and faculty.* Los Angeles, CA: Higher Education
Research Institute.

Astin, H. S., Antonio, A. L., Cress, C. M., & Astin, A. W. (1996). *Faculty involvement in community service* [Report for RAND Corporation]. Los Angeles, LA:
Higher Education Research Institute.

Baxter Magolda, M. (1999). *Creating contexts for learning and self-authorship: Constructive developmental pedagogy.* Nashville, TN: Vanderbilt University Press.

Boyte, H. (2008). Against the current: Developing the civic agency of students. *Change, 4*(3), 8–15.

Bringle, R. G., & Hatcher, J. A. (1996). Implementing service learning in higher education. *Journal of Higher Education, 67*(2), 67–73.

Chickering, A. (1998). Why we should encourage student activism. *About Campus 2*(6), 2–3.

Chickering, A. W., & Gamson, Z. (1999). Development and adaptations of the seven principles for good practice in undergraduate education. *New Directions for Teaching and Learning,* 80, 75–81.

Chickering, A., & Reisser, L. (1993). *Education and identity* (2nd ed.). San Francisco: Jossey-Bass.

Cress, C., Burack, C., Giles, D. E., Jr., Elkins, J., & Stevens, M. (2010). *A promising connection: Increasing college access and success through civic engagement.* Boston, MA: Campus Compact.

Dewey, J. (1916). *Democracy and education.* New York, NY: The Free Press.

Eyer, J., & Giles, D., Jr. (1999). *Where's the learning in service-learning?* San Francisco, CA: Jossey-Bass.

Gamson, Z. (2000). Defining the civic agenda for higher education. In T. Ehrlich (Ed.), *Civic responsibility and higher education* (pp. 367–372). Phoenix, AZ: Oryx Press.

Heifetz, R. (1994). *Leadership without easy answers.* Cambridge, MA: Harvard University Press.

Indiana University-Purdue University Indiana Task Force on Civic Engagement. (2004). *Doubling the numbers: Civic engagement task force report.* Retrieved from http://www.iupui.edu/~fcouncil/documents/civic.htm.

Keeling, R. (Ed.). (2004). *Learning reconsidered.* Washington, DC: American College Personnel Association and National Association of Student Affairs Professionals.

Kolb, D. (1984). *Experiential learning: Experience as the source of learning and development.* Englewood Cliffs, NJ: Prentice Hall.

Komives, S., Longerbeam, S., Mainella, F., & Osteen, L. (2005). Leadership identity development model: Applications from grounded theory. *Journal of College Student Development, 46*(6), 593–611.

Kouzes, J., & Posner, B. (2008). *The leadership challenge* (4th ed). San Francisco, CA: Jossey-Bass.

McIntosh, H., Hart, D., & Youniss, J. (2007). The influence of family political discussion on youth civic development: Which parent qualities matter? *American Political Science Association Journal, 40*(3), 495–499.

Parks, S. (2000). *Big questions, worthy dreams.* San Francisco CA: Jossey-Bass.

Peet, M. (2011). *Integrative knowledge and learning: Theory, research and practice.* Ann Arbor: University of Michigan.

Putnam, R. D. (2000). *Bowling alone.* New York, NY: Simon & Schuster.

Rudolph, F. (1990). *The American college and university: A history.* Athens: University of Georgia Press.

Rudolph, F. (1991). *The American college and university: A history.* Athens, GA: University of Georgia Press.

Vogelgesang, L. J., & Astin, A. W. (2000). Comparing the effects of community service and service-learning. *Michigan Journal of Community Service Learning,* 7(1), 25–34.

Wheatley, M. (2007). *Finding our way: Leadership for an uncertain time.* San Francisco, CA: Berrett- Koehler.

Zull, J. (2006). Key aspects of how the brain learns. *New Directions for Adult and Continuing Education,* 110, 3–10.

11

TEACHING FOR TRANSFORMATION IN BUSINESS EDUCATION

Sarah Stookey

I didn't pay all this tuition to learn to teach little kids.

—Student taking Ethics and
Social Issues for Managers course

This student comment was feedback at the end of a required management course. The activity he referred to was a project working with local middle schoolers. Halfway through a semester-long course on business and social issues, the business students began a six-week process of collaboration with younger students on campus and in the middle school to understand basic principles of business organization and the relationship between business and society. Working in small groups, the business students were charged with developing and implementing lesson plans for the younger children. The collaboration culminated in the creation of a rudimentary business plan for a fantasy business of the children's choosing and an on-campus *Business Idol* competition in front of a panel of judges. Was this a legitimate form of education? What should business students learn, and how should they learn it? As a professor of management, how can I move my teaching toward transformation and learning? In this chapter I reflect on my experience grappling with these questions.

Earlier in this book Fried calls for a fundamental reworking of the mental architecture in higher education. She describes the prevailing divide between student and academic affairs as conceptual and organizational segregation that subverts the pressing project of preparing students for engaged citizenship. Student affairs activities teach students to organize, serve, and interact in areas of common interest, whether it is Christianity, paintball, or politics. Students take responsibility for identifying issues, establishing strategies, recruiting participants, forming alliances with partners, marshaling resources, and organizing themselves. In contrast, when students enroll in academic courses they are typically far more passive and are expected to facilitate other people's inscrutable agendas. For students in the United States the Great Recession and the broader globalized social and environmental crisis highlights the deficiencies of this segregated model of higher education. How can we provide alternatives that more effectively prepare students for these challenges by integrating the self-directed and collaborative action more commonly found in cocurricular activities with academic learning?

The student's comment at the beginning of this chapter showcases how perceptions of higher education in general and the academic/cocurricular divide in particular play out in business schools. The student's conception of legitimate education, centered on a particular set of academic experiences involving classrooms, lectures, quizzes, and papers, was compromised by work with middle schoolers. Having absorbed the ideological and economic views that higher education is a market commodity, he was willing to pay to consume a legitimate educational product. But off-campus work where he was expected to design and implement a learning process with 13-year-olds felt like community service or a club activity. By definition this made it seem nonacademic, noneducational—not worth paying for.

Readers of this book whose academic homes are in other parts of the university may also consider a business school classroom an unlikely or even inappropriate place to attempt to integrate academic and nonacademic efforts. Earlier in this book Fried laments the model of higher education that marries principles of Roman bureaucracy and mass assembly production systems. If there's any place on campus such a narrowly functionalist mind-set would prevail it would seem to be in the business school. Business education is generally understood to be narrowly instrumental, focused on developing the very particular skills of dominant business practice (Giacalone & Thompson, 2006). Given the ways organizational, economic, and cultural practices promoted in business schools have been direct causes of immense suffering and injustice (including but clearly predating the latest economic crisis), it could be reasonably argued that business schools should be written off by those interested in transformative education. Some in the academic community would argue that at their best, business schools are financially necessary adjuncts to the real educational work of arts and sciences, helping to subsidize university operations. At their worst they suck resources and force reorientation of economics and other fields in function of advancing business interests. The possibility of their being part of a revitalization of higher education seems not only unlikely but disingenuous.

My teaching is based on the conviction that commitment to socially useful education *requires* working in and with business schools, and that it can be done usefully. But I also recognize the very substantial obstacles that stand in the way.

Why Business Education Matters

One could argue that business education matters by virtue of numbers: It is by far the most popular major in U.S. colleges and universities, enrolling over 20% of all students (Glenn, 2011). But the primary reason business education matters is that it is the training ground for business people who are members of the primary organizational unit of the economy. The economy is a fundamental social process. Any doubts about the social impact of business have been decisively challenged by the financial collapse and the resulting Great Recession that has caused a reorganization of social relationships throughout American society and begun to reframe some American values. The political economy of our times is a relatively recent variant of capitalism, often referred to as *managerial*, in which the decision-making authority of top management predominates (Chandler, 1984). Pursuing social transformation requires more than rejecting the effects of managerial capitalism. It requires understanding how economic organizations operate and how they can be oriented; this is the focus of business education.

Business education matters because it is part of the path taken by the people who seek to become the managers who will make the decisions that will affect our livelihoods and economic lives. As a whole, business courses advance concepts, agendas, and techniques that tend to subvert the larger social good (Zohar & Marshall, 2004). For example, it is generally assumed that profit maximization is the sole and undeniable goal of business, and that those organizations that make the most profits are the best models of success.

This assumption shapes what students are taught about employment practices, marketing strategies, financial systems, and so forth. It also shapes how they are taught. It is assumed that prevailing business practices are profitable, effective (faith in market mechanism dictates they wouldn't prevail if they weren't effective), and, therefore, legitimate. In this context, business education exemplifies the functionalist qualities Kant attributed to universities: "to produce well-educated bureaucrats to manage the emerging nation-states, and to create knowledge for emerging industry that was based on the application of scientific information to industrial problems" (Kant, 1798/1979). The effectiveness of business education is thus generally measured by the degree to which it transmits seemingly absolute (and apparently objective) knowledge validated by apparently unimpeachable external authorities.

The apparent authority of this educational model is reinforced by the mandates of the accrediting body, the Association to Advance Collegiate Schools of Business (Pfeffer & Fong, 2002). This has implications for doctoral training, hiring, research programs, promotion and tenure processes, and institutional strategy. It also affects the ways business students perceive their educational experience. While a functionalist and passive model of education surely operates in other disciplines, it is particularly powerful in business schools because of the composition of the student body. Undergraduate students who major in business are more likely than their peers in other disciplines to be from working-class and recent immigrant families, and therefore first-generation college students (Green, 1992; Leppel, 2001). Especially during an economic crisis these students are more likely than their peers in the arts and sciences, for example, to perceive college education as preparation for a marketable career.

If it seems a certain educational content is what has been ratified by the organizations and managers who will hire students when they graduate, then the more apparently straightforward the transmission of that content, the better it will seem to these students. Learning processes that seem to divert time and energy from the transmission and absorption of such content is perceived as a misuse of student time and, as the student's comment at the beginning of this chapter indicates, money. The processes of transformative learning are a problem in multiple ways. Emphasis on self-direction can seem to undercut the authority attributed to the professor but also the business establishment and whole political-economic system. Emphasis on engaging with local and often marginalized people can seem to subvert progress toward affiliation with powerful business interests. Emphasis on interaction can seem to undermine progress toward technical knowledge. Emphasis on critical analysis of underlying assumptions can seem to detract from developing expertise in the tools of power. For these and other reasons, students can be the most powerful source of resistance to teaching toward transformation.

Teaching Toward Transformation in the Management Classroom

While a business school classroom presents substantial obstacles to transformative teaching and learning, it also provides important opportunities. Most powerfully, the explicit subject of business education is business. The clear and powerful role of business in society and in individuals' lives provides endless openings for connecting concepts, theories, and techniques with real-world consequences and with thinking about possibilities for action. For example, the mortgage-related financial collapse of 2008 and its often powerful effects on students' lives (as they or their parents lost jobs and struggled with mortgage payments) could be considered in terms of the kinds of business and management techniques students were used to thinking about in classes (i.e., finance). But it also required analysis of changes in the structure of the U.S. economy in the past 30 years (including the extent and cause of declining real wages, systems of credit, etc.) and the globalization of finance.

In my experience it is not easy to get students to actively evaluate, either in classroom discussions or writing assignments, what they believe are the inviolable tenets of business operating procedures, such as profit must be maximized, labor is a cost—to be reduced—of business, or taxes are an unnecessary drain on business. This kind of thinking fundamentally challenges students' conception of what business education is supposed to be. It requires them to read authors from disciplines, eras, and places they are not only unfamiliar with but that they consider peripheral. It also requires them to consider their lived experience as a legitimate source of knowledge that might be used to shape organizational or social policies. Business students have particularly compelling expertise in the political economy, especially as compared to their peers in other disciplines. As a group they are likely to have greater firsthand knowledge of work, business, and the painful effects of managerial capitalism. However, these same characteristics often mean that business students are likely to be less accustomed to analytic and interdisciplinary education. They are less likely to feel comfortable reading, discussing, and writing about materials and ideas that are not explicitly about business. They are more likely to have been encouraged to be passive participants in the classroom. In addition to unfamiliar reading, discussions, and writing assignments, when they are asked to work with little kids in a local middle school, their nervousness about the quality of the educational product they're making a significant sacrifice to acquire may become intense.

For business students being required to move beyond the familiar academic routines of their classrooms in these ways is fundamentally about developing a more comprehensive understanding of social interdependencies. It is part of the larger effort to encourage them to consider the norms and practices of business in terms of a broader set of interests than simply profit maximization. It is about giving them opportunities to collaborate with the kinds of people they are not used to working with. And it's about asserting the value of their own abilities to articulate goals and interests, develop strategies, and lead. All these considerations have the potential to transform the students' worldview by forcing or encouraging them to view the world and their own behavior from a much broader perspective. This is not the typical approach of standard business education. These kinds of critiques often appear as the purview of student affairs because they are crucial to common well-being and arise beyond the focus of specific disciplines.

Conclusion

As Fried asserts in Chapter 1, p. 7, "Dismantling mental architecture is difficult." It may be particularly difficult in a business school. But I believe there are urgent reasons to try and reasons to hope. As educators seeking social transformation, we can't afford the luxury of writing business off. Business school professors need to seek ways of developing engaged citizens with broad social perspectives. Crossing the academic/student affairs divide is risky. Often our students will resist, and we will need to consider their reservations carefully. The student's comment at the beginning of this chapter represents sentiments we need to respond to. But we need to be willing to press ahead, experimenting and innovating. The status quo does not serve us well because it enhances the inequities of the managerial system and does not provide alternative approaches to redressing them.

And often, as an added bonus, we will find students respond quite positively to being pushed in these ways because of their occasional needs for redress. Another student involved in the same project wrote:

> Hi professor . . . I didn't have time to explain some of my thoughts and relevance about the class. Your idea about how to do this project was great. Me being a minority and interacting with the students with similar backgrounds worked out well. In relation to the class I believed I learned a lot as you will read in my paper. I think that during the first 3 months I was writing so many papers and reading about 200 pages in the books that I was definetly [*sic*] feeling some pressure in the class. So I believe [giving] us a chance to teach these younger students worked out in having all that information sink in for me and teach something new to student[s] who new [*sic*] nothing about what we learn. I believe you should continue with your great idea because you bring something different than any other class I have taken in my 4 and [a] half years here. Well I just wanted to express how I felt about everything as you will read on my paper.

References

Chandler, A., Jr. (1984). The emergence of managerial capitalism. *Business History Review, 58*(4), 473–503. Retrieved from http://www.jstor.org/stable/3114162

Giacalone, R. A., & Thompson, K. R. (2006). Business ethics and social responsibility education: Shifting the worldview. *Academy of Management Learning & Education, 5*(3), 266–277.

Glenn, D. (2011). The default major: Skating through business school. *New York Times.* Retrieved from http://www.nytimes.com/2011/04/17/education/edlife/edl17business-t.html

Green, K. C. (1992). *After the boom: Management majors in the 1990s.* New York, NY: McGraw-Hill.

Kant, I. (1979). *The conflict of the faculties/Der streit der fakultaten* (M. Gregor, Trans.). New York, NY: Abaris Books. (Original work published 1798)

Leppel, K. (2001). Race, Hispanic ethnicity, and the future of the college business major in the United States. *Journal of Education for Business, 76*(4), 209–216.

Pfeffer, J., & Fong, C. T. (2002). The end of business schools? Less success than meets the eye. *Academy of Management Learning & Education, 1*(1), 78–95. Retrieved from http://www.jstor.org/stable/40214102

Stookey, S. (2011). Education for integrity: Business, elitism and the liberal arts. In A. Stachowicz-Stanusch & C. Wankel (Eds.), *Management education for integrity* (pp. 193–215). Bingley, UK: Emerald Publishing.

Zohar, D., & Marshall, I. (2004). *Spiritual capital: Wealth we can live by.* London, UK: Bloomsbury.

12

ENGAGING THE HEAD AND THE HEART

Intergroup Dialogue in Higher Education

Craig John Alimo

I am sitting in my office, checking my e-mail when the phone rings. I pick up the phone. Unexpected phone calls I receive sometimes proceed something like this: "Hello, Mr. Alimo, I heard from so-and-so that you do diversity training, do you still do that?" the caller asks.

"Um . . . sure," I say with a little hesitation. "Oh great! You see, I teach this University 101 course with new students who are undeclared majors. Can you come tomorrow and do a diversity unit? Don't worry, you have about 30 minutes, so it won't take much of your time. You can just lecture to them about diversity because I have two other topics to fit in for that one-hour class. Will that work for you?"

Orientation programming and associated first-year seminars are of critical importance to student transitions to college. Fitting all the important information an incoming student should know into a program sometimes calls for an educational shoehorn. If the diversity class is to be effective, it cannot not be relegated to the "quick and dirty," something to be squeezed in. Diversity education requires time, thought, and an atmosphere of trust. We know that many if not most students have not had much opportunity to interact across racial differences (Milem & Umbach, 2004; Milem, Umbach, & Liang, 2004), and that salient elements of human diversity are not always obvious. In many cases these courses are taught by academic faculty members who have had little or no training in pedagogy, learning, or group facilitation. The skill level of faculty in these areas limits the extent and type of learning in these classes.

I have designed and facilitated a variety of social justice educational interventions over the past 13 years. The majority of these interventions have been Diversity 101 types of programs. The kind of conversation at the beginning of this chapter has been a regular occurrence. Many of these intake conversations with instructors end up being interventions prior to the class. They usually reveal the requester's lack of understanding about student learning outcomes with regard to human diversity issues. I generally offer a set of learning outcomes and then negotiate them with the instructor for a minimum of two hours so the lesson plan is developmentally appropriate.

The most obvious problem in these negotiations is that many instructors believe that learning about diversity however it is defined is like learning about quadratic equations. The diversity unit is seen as a defined amount of content to be delivered to students in about the same fashion one would deliver content in any other 101-type course. This dilemma highlights several issues in my work: Faculty members tend to have very little understanding of the learning process. They often believe that learning is exclusively cognitive and that their responsibility is limited to presenting information to students. Students' responsibility is to learn the material, an accomplishment they demonstrate by repeating it in some form. They also tend to ignore contextual issues and issues of previous life experience. The diversity unit within this framework can be dropped into any course as a person might fit a piece into a puzzle, but in this case nobody is really sure about the picture the puzzle represents, and there is little concern about whether the piece fits. My first task is to fill in the instructor on these concerns and then negotiate an appropriate amount of time to do an experiential workshop.

It is also my experience that students have been well trained to articulate conversational norms that minimize conflict in these conversations. Typically when I ask students what kinds of ground rules they might expect from one another, I get the following replies:

- "Respect."
- "Be open minded."
- "Education."
- "Don't speak when others are speaking."

These seem to be automatic rather than thoughtful responses, much like answering questions on a multiple-choice test. Many of our incoming students have had sufficient training prior to college to know what behavior is socially desirable during the diversity class. Students exhibit good behavior to the trainer so they can all get through it with a minimum of conflict. There is an unspoken consensus that diversity training is something like medicine, to be taken quickly, without tasting anything unpleasant and without worrying about outcomes. A dance between the instructor, the students, and me often takes place in the shared experience of a Diversity 101 workshop. Not all students respond as automatons, not all instructors of these types of classes are as thoughtless, and not all these interventions seem as pointless as I have described. However, all these interventions, to be effective, must engage the whole student, attend to the dynamics of the group, and help the instructor learn that social justice education requires engagement through affect, reflection, and application.

Program Design

Intergroup dialogue in higher education is a sustained social justice educational program that invites people from different social identity groups affected by a form of social oppression to examine their relationships (Zúñiga, 1998; Zúñiga, Nagda, & Sevig, 2002; Zúñiga, Nagda, Sevig, Thompson, & Dey, 1995; Zúñiga & Sevig, 1997). These programs offer necessary time and space where students meet and have informed conversation about issues regarding community, diversity, conflict, and societal change. The content of the conversation is academic and personal. For example, students engage in dialogue about a web of oppression. The conversation includes readings by Beverly Tatum (1992), an African American psychologist; Audre Lorde (1982, 1986), an African American lesbian poet; and other social justice theoreticians. Students then receive a set of cards with words and pictures that describe various aspects of oppression. The cards are sewn together in a web, and students hold the web as they identify the interconnections among oppressors and oppressed in systemic ways. The intervention is an opportunity to address issues of intergroup relations in ways that informal discussions and formal classrooms may not always provide. Informal conversations are typically uninformed about historical and other academically relevant issues. Formal academic conversations typically exclude emotional reactions or do not help students process their reactions and conflicts. Participants in intergroup dialogue discussions learn about social issues, gain confidence in discussing them, and develop skills to address these issues in their communities. They are encouraged to engage in conversations in which they are not continuing to practice rhetoric or debate but are seeking to understand one another. These types of conversations are not an exercise in rhetoric or competition but a practice in building positive relationships in an intergroup setting by learning how to create empathy among all members of the group in an egalitarian setting (Zúñiga, Nagda, & Sevig). As such, they demonstrate integrative, transformative learning. They always involve emotional engagement and usually require behavioral change. Ultimately the goal of these interventions is to help participants reframe their ideas about their own place in the world and their relationships with others who are different. These types of interventions take time to conduct and even more time to process.

Intergroup dialogue is also different from other forms of social justice education in that it is a sustained experience that has a significant amount of academic content (Zúñiga et al., 2002). This experience has greater scope and depth than Diversity 101 interventions. The format varies from 6 to 15 weeks with two to three hours of face-to-face contact per session. Time is needed for participants to acquire new knowledge and to develop relationships. In the context of honest relationships, participants can take the perspectives and reactions of others into account. After this kind of activity students are given the opportunity to discuss their reactions and to reflect in written form on their place in the web, their feelings, and any sort of action that seems appropriate for them to consider in response to these insights. Since the 1950s, social psychologists and educators have documented the importance of creating optimal conditions, like extended contact between groups, for reducing bias and prejudice (Allport, 1954). Modern neuroscientists have also examined how extended time and contact assists in the reduction of activity in the fight-and-flight-triggered amygdala activity and associated cortisol hormone production in the brain when engaged in cross-race interactions (Page-Gould, Mendoza-Denton, & Tropp, 2008; Phelps et al., 2000).

Intergroup dialogue focuses on the process of the dialogues themselves and on learning outcomes. Readings and brief lectures focus on the social dynamics of difference and domination, as well as the dynamics that develop between participants in the group. The dialogues are places where a number of challenging activities can happen so that students of differing groups can start to question different preconceptions they have about one another. Students can engage in self-reflection, challenging the ignorance or lack of information they may have about other groups or themselves. In this self-reflection, students can come to new insights and even participate in the discovery of identities they may never have considered before (Zúñiga et al., 1995). Zúñiga (1998) requires ongoing conversation among facilitators in order for the facilitators to reflect on their internal dynamics as well as the dynamics of the dialogue group.

The process involves a four-stage progression necessary for successful intergroup dialogue in higher education programs (Zúñiga et al., 2002). The stages, which are listed here, highlight a pedagogical structure for organizing intergroup dialogue in higher education curricula.

1. *Group beginnings.* Students meet and build relationships with others in the group, focusing on homogeneous social identity groups and dialogues between groups.
2. *Exploring differences and commonalities of experience.* Students engage in self-exploration about the nature of difference and dominance, as well as the effects of institutional context.
3. *Exploring and talking about issues of conflict.* Students discuss hot topics between social identity groups, and conversations typically shift from friendly to more controversial or heated. Skills developed during the first two stages are practiced as a matter of developing understanding and respect among groups with different perspectives.
4. *Action planning and alliance building.* Students, individually and collectively, begin to plan actions and behaviors that contribute to the elimination of the manifestation of oppression explored in the dialogue. Participants may make individual commitments to work toward personal education, work with another person in their social identity group or across identity difference on acquiring more information about a particular manifestation of oppression, or work with others on an action project like a workshop for peers in a residence hall.

These dialogues involve three principles of practice:

1. *Maintaining a social justice lens.* This focus is necessary to observe the connections between oppressive dynamics that exist throughout

personal, cultural, and institutional levels of oppression (Katz, 1978). All participants must feel equal in these dialogues to implement one of Allport's (1954) conditions to create an optimal environment for bias reduction. Intergroup dialogue uses two cofacilitators, one of whom should possess membership in at least one of the social identity groups that are salient in the dialogue.

2. *Attending to process and content.* Intergroup dialogue attends to the content the dialogue addresses (e.g., racism, sexism, or other isms) and the group dynamics or process of the participants in the dialogue.

3. *Actualizing praxis—reflection and action—in dialogue.* In the spirit of Freire (1970/1993), intergroup dialogue would not be genuine dialogue unless there was some sort of cycling between self-reflection and developing action steps for the future. The acquisition of information and the focus on skill development are necessary components (Zúñiga, Nagda, Chesler, & Cytron-Walker, 2007).

These four stages and three practice principles set intergroup dialogue in higher education apart from other forms of dialogue. The stages offer support for students in learning content and in developing relationships within and between the groups involved. Intergroup dialogue is a form of social justice education, as the practice principles encompass many of its features such as its social critique, the balance between content and process, as well as the reflective action it encourages.

Although intergroup dialogue has been recognized by a number of professional organizations as an innovative practice (American Association for Higher Education, National Association for Student Personnel Administrators, & American College Personnel Association, 1998; Hurtado, Milem, Clayton-Pedersen, & Allen, 1999; Tatum, 1992), it is not without limitations. Programs like intergroup dialogue that address social oppression are viewed by some as limiting individuals' personal expression, as well as part of a larger educational agenda to indoctrinate college students with politically liberal ideas (National Association of Scholars [NAS], 2008). Members of NAS and other organizations tend to view their programs as doctrinaire rather than educational.

Research on Intergroup Dialogue in Higher Education

Since the development of intergroup dialogue in higher education at the University of Michigan in the early 1990s, efforts have been made to evaluate its impact. Studies address a number of topics such as course content (Lopez, Gurin, & Nagda, 1998) and forms of action (Alimo, 2010; Gurin, Nagda, & Lopez, 2004; Nagda, Kim, & Truelove, 2004; Zúñiga, Williams, & Berger, 2005). Extant research on intergroup dialogue informs researchers and student affairs professionals about some of the ways in which participation in intergroup dialogue programs yields a number of positive outcomes, including increased knowledge about multicultural issues (Geranios, 1997; Vasques Scalera, 1999), and comfort, honesty, and trust between participants (Yeakley, 1998; for additional information about research on program impacts and training in program implementation, contact me at calimo@berkeley.edu).

Epilogue

A few summers ago during a research meeting at Syracuse University, I was fortunate enough to hear some students speak about the multiple ways their participation in an intergroup dialogue had an impact on them. These students did not tell stories of how they were dragged to a mandatory diversity workshop or forced to sit in a Diversity 101 presentation. This small sample of students from around the country had participated in programs designed and executed in a manner similar to what is described in this chapter. Students of color spoke of how involvement in intergroup dialogue helped connect them to the institution, how the conversations gave them hope and empowered them to work with people in similar and differing racial groups to work toward ending forms of bias and discrimination. These students also acknowledged that having a community like those created via the intergroup dialogue programs kept them enrolled as students at their colleges and universities, even when they considered leaving. A number of students from privileged groups acknowledged how they learned about students who acted differently with them and that they learned that less privileged students changed their behavior when they were with more privileged students in order to improve their chances of acceptance. This caused the privileged students to learn a significant amount about themselves and their effect on others.

Participation in these programs created spaces that were not always safe but challenged students to build relationships across differences and learn to work with others in tough conversations. In short, they learned about justice and injustice by understanding their own place in societal hierarchies, the status of their own and other key groups, and the historical and cultural context that has produced these circumstances. Finally they learned that praxis as the integration of theory and practice allows people to identify oppressive phenomena and challenge them for the welfare of their communities (Freire, 1970/1993).

References

Alimo, C. J. (2010). *From dialogue to action: The development of White racial allies* (Doctoral dissertation, University of Maryland). Retrieved from http://drum.lib .umd.edu/handle/1903/11111

Allport, G. W. (1954). *The nature of prejudice.* Cambridge, MA: Addison-Wesley.

American Association for Higher Education, National Association for Student Personnel Administrators, & American College Personnel Association. (1998). *Powerful partnerships: A shared responsibility for learning.* Retrieved from http:// www.myacpa.org/pub/documents/taskforce.pdf

Freire, P. (1993). *Pedagogy of the oppressed* (M. B. Ramos, Trans.). New York, NY: Continuum. (Original work published 1970)

Geranios, C. A. (1997). *Cognitive, affective, and behavioral outcomes of multicultural courses and intergroup dialogues in higher education* (Doctoral dissertation). Retrieved from ProQuest Dissertations and Theses database. (UMI No. 9725294)

Gurin, P., Nagda, B. A., & Lopez, G. E. (2004). The benefits of diversity in education for democratic citizenship. *Journal of Social Issues, 60*(1), 17–34. doi: 10.1111/ j.0022-4537.2004.00097.x

Hurtado, S. (2001). Research and evaluation on intergroup dialogue. In D. Schoem & S. Hurtado, S., Milem, J. F., Clayton-Pedersen, A. R., & Allen, W. R. (1999). *Enacting diverse learning environments: Improving the climate for racial/ethnic diversity in higher education.* Washington, DC: Graduate School of Education and Human Development, George Washington University.

Katz, J. H. (1978). *White awareness: Handbook for anti-racism training.* Norman: University of Oklahoma Press.

Lopez, G. E., Gurin, P., & Nagda, B. A. (1998). Education and understanding structural causes for group inequalities. *Political Psychology, 19(2),* 305–329. doi: 10.1111/ 0162-895X.00106

Lorde, A. (1982). *Chosen poems—old and new.* New York, NY: Norton.

Lorde, A. (1986). *Our dead behind us.* New York, NY: Norton.

Milem, J. F., Umbach, P., & Liang, C. T. H. (2004). Exploring the perpetuation hypothesis: The role of colleges and universities in desegregating society. *Journal of College Student Development, 45*(6), 688–700. doi: 10.1353/csd.2004.0070

Nagda, B. A., Kim, C.-w., & Truelove, Y. (2004). Learning about difference, learning with others, learning to transgress. *Journal of Social Issues, 60(1),* 195–214. doi: 10.1111/j.0022-4537.2004.00106.x

National Association of Scholars. (2008). *Rebuilding campus community: The wrong imperative.* Retrieved from http://www.nas.org/polStatements.cfm

Page-Gould, E., Mendoza-Denton, R., & Tropp, L. R. (2008). With a little help from my cross-group friend: Reducing anxiety in intergroup contexts through cross-group friendship. *Journal of Personality and Social Psychology, 95*(5), 1080–1094. doi: 10.1037/0022-3514.95.5.1080

Phelps, E. A., O'Connor, K. J., Cunningham, W. A., Funayama, E. S., Gatenby, J. C., Gore, J. C., & Banaji, M. R. (2000). Performance on indirect measures of race evaluation predicts amygdala activation. *Journal of Cognitive Neuroscience, 12,* 729–238. doi: 10.1162/089892900562552

Tatum, B. D. (1992). Talking about race, learning about racism: The application of racial identity development theory in the classroom. *Harvard Educational Review, 62*(1), 1–24. doi: 0017-8055/92/0200-0001

Vasques Scalera, C. M. (1999). *Democracy, diversity, dialogue: Education for critical multicultural citizenship* (Doctoral dissertation). Available from ProQuest Dissertations and Theses database. (UMI No. 9959879)

Yeakley, A. M. (1998). *The nature of prejudice change: Positive and negative change processes arising from intergroup contact experiences* (Doctoral dissertation). Retrieved from ProQuest Dissertations and Theses database. (UMI No. 9910030)

Zúñiga, X. (1998). Fostering intergroup dialogue on campus: Essential ingredients. *Diversity Digest.* Retrieved from http://www.diversityweb.org/Digest/W98/fostering.html

Zúñiga, X., Nagda, B. A., Chesler, M., & Cytron-Walker, A. (Eds.). (2007). *Intergroup dialogue in higher education: Meaningful learning about social justice.* Washington, DC: Association for the Study of Higher Education.

Zúñiga, X., Nagda, B. A., & Sevig, T. D. (2002). Intergroup dialogues: An educational model for cultivating engagement across differences. *Equity & Excellence in Education, 35*(1), 7–17. doi: 10.1080/713845248

Zúñiga, X., Nagda, B. A., Sevig, T. D., Thompson, M., & Dey, E. (1995, November). *Speaking the unspeakable: Student learning outcomes in intergroup dialogues on a college campus.* Paper presented at the annual conference of the Association for the Study of Higher Education, Orlando, Florida.

Zúñiga, X., & Sevig, T. D. (1997). Bridging the "us/them" divide through intergroup dialogue and peer leadership. *The Diversity Factor, 6*(2), 23–28.

Zúñiga, X., & Sevig, T. D. (2000). Bridging the "us/them" divide through intergroup dialogue and peer leadership. In M. Adams, W. J. Blumenfeld, R. Castañeda, H. W. Hackman, M. L. Peters, & X. Zúñiga (Eds.), *Readings for diversity and social justice: An anthology on racism, antisemitism, sexism, heterosexism, ableism and classism* (pp. 488–493). New York, NY: Routledge.

Zúñiga, X., Williams, E. A., & Berger, J. B. (2005). Action-oriented democratic outcomes: The impact of student involvement with campus diversity. *Journal of College Student Development, 46*(6), 660–678. doi: 10.1353/csd.2005.0069

13

FIRST-YEAR EXPERIENCE

Practice and Process

Christopher Pudlinski and Scott Hazan

P eer mentors have been a powerful element in helping students become engaged with their own learning process. Peer mentors in the program described in this chapter take a Peer Leadership Seminar that specifically prepares them to perform this function. The course helps the peer mentors learn the roles they play in the first-year experience (FYE) classes and the skills they need to perform this role effectively The following story is fairly typical. A student in the peer mentor class had signed up to be the student manager of a Division 1 athletic team at our university. The work and the hours expected of her were greater than she anticipated, and she was having trouble keeping up with her schoolwork. The student confided to her peer mentor that she felt overwhelmed. The peer mentor used the wise choice model (Downing, 2011), taught in the Peer Leadership Seminar, to help the student take ownership of the issue and decide what to do. The wise choice process consists of six questions: What's my present situation? How would I like my situation to be? What are my possible choices? What's the likely outcome of each possible choice? Which choice(s) will I commit to doing? and When and how will I evaluate my plan?

The student recognized she had two nonoptimal choices: She could continue with her position as manager of the basketball team (and let her grades continue to slip), or she could resign from her position and be left with a feeling of failure and hesitation about getting involved in future activities. Since the student felt comfortable enough to confide in her peer mentor, the mentor was able to talk with her about the positive aspects of being an involved student but also the importance of balance and finding a level of involvement that allows her to be successful in all areas of college life. After a few conversations the student decided she could not keep up the current pace and resigned from being the manager of the team.

If the story ended here you might say our peer mentoring program was unsuccessful in involving a first-year student in cocurricular activities. We now have a student who chose to get involved, became overwhelmed, and may be hesitant about getting involved again. The story did not end there. During the initial conversations about her involvement, the student and the peer mentor developed a relationship and built a level of trust. They continued to learn about each other and explore other opportunities for involvement. The peer mentor was a student government association (SGA) senator, which stimulated the student's interest in SGA. She decided to go to a few SGA meetings to see what it was all about. The student realized the impact she could have by participating in student government. Before jumping in, she spoke at length with her peer mentor about the time commitment and the level of involvement. After careful consideration she decided this position would be a perfect balance for her. She ran for SGA senator during the spring election, won her seat, and is now an involved student who feels connected to the university and her peer mentor. She is confident she will be successful as she starts her sophomore year this fall. This student is just one of the success stories from our peer mentoring program.

Building upon this story, this chapter highlights the success of the peer mentor program at our university how it builds upon a collaboration between student affairs and academic affairs. By using the FYE course, which all students take, the program creates a collaborative project between academic and student affairs staff members.

How and why does the collaboration between student affairs and academic affairs work with our peer mentors? The collaborative pieces of this project are two presemester training sessions and the peer mentor class, both collaboratively designed by representatives from academic affairs and student affairs. The purpose of training is to orient the peers to role expectations for themselves and their faculty member and to discuss the collaborative process in the FYE classroom. Peer mentors are expected to understand and become comfortable with the professor's teaching style, to apply their leadership skills in the classroom, and to act as extended orientation leaders for FYE students.

Peer mentors attended a biweekly class in which they discussed pedagogy, leadership, and support for student engagement. The peers read and discussed articles about pedagogy and leadership throughout the semester and were required to design a detailed lesson plan for a lesson or activity they would conduct in their assigned FYE class section. In the Peer Leadership Seminar, each student made a presentation and submitted a final paper summarizing his or her experience in the FYE class (see an example of a syllabus in the Appendix). Having a faculty member and student affairs professional with differing university experiences and perspectives coteach the Peer Leadership Seminar allowed for varied and nuanced discussion of mentors' problems and concerns. Student affairs professionals, unlike most faculty members, bring greater knowledge of residence life issues, clubs and organizations, campus events and resources, and student leadership skills and opportunities to these classroom discussions.

The Program

FYE programs are an excellent place for collaboration between student affairs and academic affairs. According to the 2009 National Survey of First-Year Seminars, teaching responsibility for FYE classes is often split among full-time faculty (61% of surveyed universities) and student affairs professionals (48%). Part-time faculty (46%) and other campus professionals (30%) also teach these classes. With respondents able to mark more than one category, it is clear that most universities, unlike ours, do not exclusively use faculty for teaching FYE courses (University of South Carolina, 2009).

While academic faculty at our university are solely responsible for their FYE classes (e.g., syllabi, tests, lectures, assignments), student affairs professionals are invited (in limited numbers) into these FYE classes to provide guest lectures (e.g., time management) and to introduce students to various campus resources. However, the Peer Leadership Seminar is unique, with an academic faculty member and the director of student activities and leadership development equally responsible for course design and content.

At our university, coteaching the required Peer Leadership Seminar began as a way to lessen faculty overload and has turned into a very sensible way to work with peer mentors. With FYE classes still exclusively taught by faculty, collaboration between student affairs staff members and academic faculty in training peer mentors became a means of bringing student affairs skills into the program. Peer mentors who are successful student leaders coteach with faculty members and provide a unique and valued perspective in a typical FYE class.

One main goal of the peer mentor program is to help involve students in the university community during their first semester. According to Astin's (1984) theory of involvement,

> Students learn more the more they are involved in both the academic and social aspects of the collegiate experience. Students who are involved devote significant energy to academics, spend time on campus, participate actively in student organizations and activities, and interact often with faculty. On the other hand, uninvolved students neglect their studies, spend little time on campus, abstain from extracurricular activities, and rarely initiate contact with faculty or other students. (Hunt, 2003, p. 133)

The most influential types of involvement are "academic involvement, involvement with faculty, and involvement with student peer groups" (Astin, 1996, p. 126). With this theory in mind we have designed a program that supports collaboration. Our comprehensive university recognizes the importance of the learning that takes place outside the classroom and that engaging students in the first semester is critical to their success. Having a student connect with a faculty member, get a job on campus, or join a club in the first semester will give that student a sense of belonging to the university and improve long-term prospects for persistence to graduation.

Program Outcomes

This FYE program is designed to help students adjust to university life, become involved in campus activities and resources, develop survival skills for college success, and become self-motivated, independent learners. Our peer mentoring program has been very successful in meeting two specific learning outcomes: helping first-year students understand how to navigate the academic and financial requirements of the university and helping them adjust to campus life. However, additional work is still needed with campus engagement, as only 61% of students feel they have a "strong [or moderate] sense of belonging to our university community." Nonetheless, students who had a peer mentor in their FYE section were much more likely to be able to explain the general education program, log onto our online undergraduate degree evaluation system, and build stronger relationships with faculty members. In this way, peers helped us better achieve our overall outcomes of the FYE program (versus sections without peer mentors) in a program assessment completed by 954 of our 1,350 first-year students in fall 2010. Overall, a key benefit noted by many first-year students was how peer mentors integrated a different perspective into the FYE class. Professors don't know about a lot of things that occur on campus. A first-year student commented: "Having a peer who knows the workings of the school is very important and useful to me. Professors are nice, but it's more relaxing and feels more relevant to talk to fellow students" (M. Funaro, personal communication, December 2010).

Finally, the most satisfying part of this collaboration is hearing the success stories from the peer mentors. During the discussion portion of the peer mentor class we encouraged the peer mentors to share their stories. One of them describes the class clown and how she was able to get him to be a productive member of the class. This first-year student "Jim" had not yet made the transition from high school, was disruptive in class, had nothing positive to contribute, and acted as if he did not want to be in the class at all. Jim was not at all connected to college expectations, and the peer mentor struggled to make a connection. She and the professor were concerned for this student and his success not only in this class but in his overall college experience. One day the student brought his guitar to class. The peer mentor noticed and took the opportunity to ask him about his interest in music. For the first time she felt he was being real with her. She asked him if at the end of class he would play a song for the class, and he did. When he started to play everyone was impressed with his ability to play and sing. Jim sang a song he wrote about a friend who had passed away. After the class the peer leader was able to talk with him about how important his music was. She had finally found a way to connect with him. He slowly became more involved in group discussions and was no longer disruptive in class. The peer, with guidance from the student affairs professional, was also able to explore with him all the opportunities he had on campus to play music. Although we do not know what the next three years will hold for him, he clearly made a connection to his peer mentor and the FYE faculty member. This connection is likely to improve his chances of overall success during his college experience (Astin, 1984).

Collaboration between academic affairs and student affairs staff members is essential to the success of this program. In this pilot year, peer leaders were involved in only 15 of 65 FYE sections. In ensuing years we expect to expand the peer leadership program and accumulate data on student success. We hope we will see improvements in students' first-semester grade point averages and in campus and community engagement. Additional collaborations are being initiated for fall 2011, including pairing an academic adviser with an FYE faculty member in FYE classes for undeclared students, with an additional emphasis on personality assessments and career planning, taught by the academic adviser.

References

Astin, A. W. (1984). Student involvement: A developmental theory for higher education. *Journal of College Student Personnel, 25*, 297–808.

Astin, A. W. (1996). Involvement in learning revisited: Lessons we have learned. *Journal of College Student Development, 37*, 123–134.

Downing, S. (2011). *On course: Strategies for creating success in college and in life.* Boston, MA: Wadsworth.

Hunt, S. K. (2003). Encouraging student involvement: An approach to teaching communication. *Communication Studies, 54*, 133–136.

University of South Carolina. (2009). *2009 National Survey of First-Year Seminars.* Retrieved from http://sc.edu/fye/research/reports/pdf/2009%20National%20Survey%20FYS_Executive%20Summary_II.pdf

FYE 301, Peer Leadership Seminar Sample Syllabus

Instructors:
Prof. Chris Pudlinski, professor, communication
Scott Hazan, director of Students Activities/Leadership Development

This course is a mixture of lecture, discussion, and a practicum (students are required to attend and actively participate in their assigned FYE 101 section).

Course Overview:

1. Participants will understand the role of peer leaders within a higher education classroom.
2. Participants will be introduced to issues of pedagogy (lesson plans, learning objectives, classroom management, active learning)
3. Participants will understand basic theories of leadership, including types and situational aspects.
4. Participants will improve their interpersonal and presentational communication skills, including speaking in a classroom setting, building peer relationships with others, and learning about peer support.
5. Because this course is about personal growth, participants should be self-reflective, honest with themselves, and open-minded (when dealing with others).

Schedule of Events (class meets every other week for 2 hours):

9/10:	Introduction to the course
	Introduction to leadership: theories, types, styles
9/24:	Leadership: theories, types, styles
	Discussion: Peers as leaders
10/8:	Personal responsibility and the wise choice process

10/22:   Basic pedagogy: Learning objectives, designing lesson plans and activities
          Theories of active learning

11/5:   More on pedagogy: What is higher education?
          Who are our first-year students?
          What does it mean to be a leader/mentor/teacher?

11/19 & 12/3: Final presentations

Requirements:

1. Attendance, preparation, and participation: This class will be a very hands-on and active learning environment. Attendance and participation in class discussions and activities are crucial to your success in this course.

2. Keeping a log: You will keep a concise and accurate log of all of your mentoring activities. You are expected to hand in these periodically over the course of the semester.

3. Desire to learn and have an open mind: Peer mentors are expected to grow and develop through this leadership process. Honest self-assessment will be an integral part of the course. Oral discussions of your own log entries will be the cornerstone of your learning experience. Peer mentors are expected to approach their work with an open mind and to be respectful of others.

4. Lesson plan: During the first week of the semester, you will consult with your FYE faculty member to determine the subject of your first classroom lecture presentation. In preparation for your first lecture you will prepare a lesson plan to be implemented in your FYE course. Lesson plans, which must reflect an understanding of class material and incorporate active learning techniques, are to be given to both your FYE 101 and 301 instructors for evaluation before they can be presented to the class.

5. Final assignment: These oral and written assignments will be based, in part, on your log entries.

REFERENCES

Abes, E., & Jones, S. (2004). Meaning-making capacity and the dynamics of lesbian college students' multiple dimensions of identity. *Journal of College Student Development, 45*(6), 612–632.

Abes, E., Jones, S., & McEwan, M. (2007). Reconceptualizing the model of multiple dimensions of identity: The role of meaning making capacity in the construction of multiple identities. *Journal of College Student Development, 48*(1), 1–22.

Allesandra, K., & Nelson, E. (2005). Identity development and self-esteem of first generation American college students: An exploratory study. *Journal of College Student Development, 46*(1), 3–13.

American Council on Education. (1937). *The student personnel point of view.* Washington, DC: Author.

American Council on Education. (1949). *The student personnel point of view* (Rev. ed.). Washington, DC: Author.

American Psychological Association. (Producer). (2005). *Working with African American clients* [DVD]. Available from http://www.apa.org/pubs/videos/4310724.aspx

Appiah, K. (2006). *Cosmopolitanism: Ethics in a world of strangers.* New York, NY: Norton.

Armstrong, K. (1993). *A history of God: Judaism, Christianity and Islam.* New York, NY: Knopf.

Aronowitz, H., & Giroux, H. (1994). *Postmodern education.* Minneapolis: University of Minnesota Press.

Arum, R., & Roksa, J. (2011). *Academically adrift: Limited learning on college campuses.* Chicago, IL: University of Chicago Press.

Atkinson, D., Morten, G., & Sue, D. W. (1979). *Counseling American minorities.* Dubuque, IA: William C. Brown.

Barker, J. (1992). *The business of discovering the future.* New York, NY: HarperCollins.

Barr, M., & Fried. J. (1981). Facts, feelings and academic credit. *New Directions for Student Services, 15*, 87–102.

References are for chapters 1 through 7. The remaining chapter references are listed at the end of the corresponding chapter.

Baxter Magolda, M. (1993). *Knowing and reasoning in college.* San Francisco, CA: Jossey-Bass.

Baxter Magolda, M. (1999). *Creating contexts for learning and self-authorship: Constructive developmental pedagogy.* Nashville, TN: Vanderbilt University Press.

Baxter Magolda, M., & King, P. (Eds.) (2004). *Learning partnerships: Theory and models of practice to educate for self-authorship.* Sterling, VA: Stylus.

Belenky, M., & Stanton, A. (2000). Inequality, development and connected knowing. In J. Mezirow (Ed.), *Learning as transformation* (pp. 71–102). San Francisco, CA: Jossey-Bass.

Bellah, R., Madsen, R., Sullivan, W., Swidler, A. & Tipton, S. (1985). *Habits of the heart: Individualism and commitment in American life.* New York, NY: Harper & Rowe.

Bloom, A. (1987). *The closing of the American mind.* New York, NY: Simon & Schuster.

Bok, D. (2006). *Our underachieving colleges: A candid look at how much students learn and why they should be learning more.* Princeton, NJ: Princeton University Press.

Bordo, S. (1987). *The flight to objectivity.* Albany, NY: SUNY Press.

Caine, G., & Caine, R. (2006). Meaningful learning and the executive functions of the brain. *New Directions for Adult and Continuing Education, 110,* 53–61.

Caine, R., Caine, G., McClintic, C., & Klimek, K. (2005). *Brain/mind learning principles in action.* Thousand Oaks, CA: Corwin Press.

Caple, R. (1987). The change process in developmental theory: A self-organization paradigm, Part 1. *Journal of College Student Personnel, 28*(1), 4–11.

Caple, R. (Ed.). (1991). *Journal of College Student Development: Special Edition, 32*(5).

Capra, F. (1982). *The turning point: Science, society and the rising culture.* New York, NY: Simon & Schuster.

Carpenter, D. S. (1991). Student affairs profession: A developmental perspective. In T. Miller, R. Winston, & Associates (Eds.), *Administration and leadership in student affairs* (pp. 253–279). Muncie, IN: Accelerated Development.

Chabris, C., & Simons, D. (2009). *The invisible gorilla.* New York, NY: Random House.

Chickering, A., & Reisser, L. (1993). *Education and identity* (2nd ed.). San Francisco: Jossey-Bass.

Cose, E. (1993). *The rage of a privileged class.* New York, NY: HarperCollins.

Cowley, M. (1993). The nature of student personnel work. In A. Rentz (Ed.), *Student affairs: A profession's heritage* (pp. 43–65). Washington, DC: American College Personnel Association. (Original work published 1936)

Crookston, B. (1974). A design for an intentional democratic community. In D. DeCoster & P. Mable (Eds.), *Student development and education in college residence halls* (pp. 55–67). Washington, DC: American College Personnel Association.

Crookston, B. (1975). Milieu management. *NASPA Journal, 13*(1), 45–55.

Cross, W., Jr. (1978). The Thomas and Cross models of psychological Nigrescence. *Journal of Black Psychology, 5,* 13031.

D'Augelli, A. (1991). Gay men in college: Identity processes and adaptations. *Journal of College Student Development, 32*(2), 140–146.

Davis, A. (1989). *Rethinking alliance building.* Paper presented at a meeting of Parallels and Intersections: Unlearning racism and other forms of oppression, Iowa City, IA.

Dewey, J. (1916). *Democracy and education.* New York, NY: MacMillan.

Dewey, J. (1938). *Experience and education.* New York, NY: MacMillan.

Diamond, L., & Butterworth, M. (2008). Questioning gender and sexual identity: Dynamic links over time. *Sex Roles, 59*(5–6), 365–376. doi: 10.1007/s11199-008-9425-3

Dungy, G., & Gordon, S. (2011). The development of student affairs. In J. Schuh, S. Jones, S. Harper, & Associates (Eds.), *Student services: A handbook for the profession* (5th ed., pp. 61–79). San Francisco, CA: Jossey-Bass.

Evans, N., Forney, D., Guido, F., Patton, L., & Renn, K. (2010). *Student development in college: Theory, research and practice* (2nd ed.) San Francisco, CA: Jossey-Bass.

Feigenbaum, E. (2007). Heterosexual privilege: The political and the personal. *Hypatia, 22*(1), 1–9.

Frankena, W. (1965). *Three historical philosohies of education.* Chicago, IL: Scott, Foresman.

Freire, P. (1985). *The politics of education.* Westport, CT: Bergin & Garvey.

Freire, P. (1990). *Pedagogy of the oppressed* (M. B. Ramos, Trans.). New York, NY: Continuum. (Original work published 1970)

Freire, P. (1994). Remarks made at Northeastern University, Boston, MA.

Fried, J. (Ed.). (1981). Education for student development. *New Directions in Student Services,* 15.

Fried. J. (2007). Higher education's new playbook: *Learning Reconsidered. About Campus, 12*(1), 2–7.

Fried, J. (2010). Burns B. Crookston: Life and legacy. *Journal of Student Affairs Research and Practice, 47*(4), 483–494.

Fried, J. (2011). *Educating students for lives of purpose: Student development as the deeper teaching,* Featured speech at NASPA national Convention, Philadelphia, PA.

Fried, J., & Associates. (1995). *Shifting paradigms in student affairs: Culture, context, teaching and learning.* Alexandria, VA: American College Personnel Association; Lanham, MD: University Press of America.

Frye, M. (1990). The possibility of feminist theory. In D. L. Rhode, *Theoretical perspectives on sexual difference* (pp. 174–184). New Haven, CT: Yale University Press.

Gardner, H. (1995). *Leading minds: An anatomy of leadership*. New York, NY: Basic Books.

Gaston, P. (2010). *The challenge of Bologna*. Sterling, VA: Stylus.

Gergen, K. (1991). *The saturated self: Dilemmas of identity in contemporary life*. New York, NY: Basic Books.

Gilligan, C. (1982). *In a different voice*. Cambridge, MA: Harvard University Press.

Gilligan, C., Lyons, N., & Hanmer, T. (1990). *Making connections*. Cambridge, MA: Harvard University Press.

Giroux, H. (1981). *Ideology, culture and the process of schooling*. Philadelphia, PA: Temple University Press.

Giroux, H. (1994). Living dangerously: Identity politics and the new cultural racism. In H. Giroux & P. McLaren (Eds.), *Between borders* (pp. 29–55). New York, NY: Routledge.

Glisczinski, D. (2007). Transformative higher education: A meaningful degree of understanding. *Journal of Transformative Education, 5*(4), 317–328. doi:10.1177/1541344607312838

Goldberg, E. (2001). *The executive brain: Frontal lobes and the civilized mind*. New York, NY: Oxford University Press.

Goleman, D. (1998). *Working with emotional intelligence*. New York, NY: Bantam.

Grossberg, L. (1994). Bringin' it all back home: Pedagogy and cultural studies. In H. Giroux & P. McLaren (Eds.), *Between borders* (pp. 1–28). New York, NY: Routledge.

Hannaford, I. (1994). The idiocy of race. *Woodrow Wilson Quarterly, 17*(2), pp. 8–45.

Hanson, R. (2009). *Buddha's brain: The practical science of happiness, love and wisdom*. Oakland, CA: New Harbinger Press.

Harding, H. (1993). Rethinking standpoint in epistemology. In L. Alcoff & E. Potter (Eds.), *Feminist epistemologies* (pp. 49–82). New York, NY: Routledge.

Harding, S. (1991). *Subjectivity, experience and knowledge: An epistemology from/for rainbow politics*. Washington, DC: Society for the Study of Values in Higher Education.

Harman, W. (1988). *Global mind change*. New York, NY: Warner Books.

Harrison, F. (Ed.). (1991). *Decolonizing anthropology*. Washington, DC: Association of Black Anthropologists.

Hawley, J., & Uretsky, J. L. (2011). *Re: Heisenberg's uncertainty principle* [Online comment]. Retrieved from http://www.newton.dep.anl.gov/askasci/phy99/phy99041.htm

Heiligman, D. (2009). *Charles and Emma's leap of faith.* New York, NY: Henry Holt.

Helms, J. (1994). The conceptualization of racial identity. In E. Trickett, R. Watts, & D. Birman (Eds.), *Human diversity* (pp. 285–311). San Francisco, CA: Jossey-Bass.

Ho, D. (1995). Internalized culture, culturocentrism and transcendence. *Counseling Psychologist,* 23(1), 4–24.

Howe, N., & Strauss, W. (1993). *13th gen.* New York, NY: Vintage Books.

Ibrahim, F. (1991). Contribution of cultural world view to generic counseling and development. *Journal of Counseling and Development,* 70(1), 13–19.

Ivey, A., Ivey, M., & Simek-Morgan, L. (1993). *Counseling and psychotherapy: A multicultural perspective* (3rd ed.) Boston, MA: Allyn & Bacon.

Jensen, E. (2000). *Brain-based learning* (Rev. ed.). San Diego, CA: The Brain Store.

Johnson, S., & Taylor, K. (Eds.). (2006). The neuroscience of adult learning. *New Directions for Adult and Continuing Education,* 110.

Johnson, V. (2002). The Nguzo Saba as a foundation for African American college student development theories. *Journal of Black Studies,* 31(4), 406–422.

Kant, I. (1979). *The conflict of the faculties/Der streit der fakultaten* (M. Gregor, Trans.). New York, NY: Abaris Books. (Original work published 1798)

Keeling, R. (Ed.). (2004). *Learning reconsidered.* Washington, DC: American College Personnel Association and National Association of Student Affairs Professionals.

Keeling, R. (Ed.). (2006). *Learning reconsidered 2.* Washington, DC: American College Personnel Association, Association of College and University Housing Officers-International, Association of College Unions-International, National Academic Advising Association, National Association for Campus Activities, National Association of Student Personnel Administrators, National Intramural Recreational Sports Association.

Kegan, R. (1994). *In over our heads.* Cambridge, MA: Harvard University Press.

Kegan, R. (2000). What form transforms? A constructive developmental approach to transformative learning. In J. Mezirow (Ed.), *Learning as transformation* (pp. 35–69). San Francisco, CA: Jossey-Bass.

Kelly, G. (1955). *The psychology of personal constructs.* New York, NY: Norton.

King, P., & Kitchener, K. (1994). *Developing reflective judgment: Understanding and promoting intellectual growth and critical thinking in adolescents and adults.* San Francisco, CA: Jossey-Bass.

Kolb, D. (1984). *Experiential learning.* Englewood Cliffs, NJ: Prentice Hall.

Korten, D. (1999). *The post-corporate world: Life after capitalism.* San Francisco, CA: Berrett Koehler.

Kovel, J. (1984). *White racism: A psychohistory.* New York, NY: Columbia University Press.

Kuhn, T. (1996). *The structure of scientific revolutions* (3rd ed.). Chicago, IL: University of Chicago Press.

Lasch, C. (1979). *The culture of narcissism.* New York, NY: Norton.

Laszlo, E. (2006). *The chaos point: The world at the crossroads.* Charlottesville, VA: Hampton Roads.

Lazlo, E. (2008). *Quantum shift in the global brain.* Rochester, VT: Inner Traditions.

Levine, A. (1980). *When dreams and heroes died.* San Francisco, CA: Jossey-Bass.

Lincoln, D., & Guba, Y. (1985). *Naturalistic inquiry.* Newbury Park, CA: Sage.

Literte, P. (2010). Revising race: How biracial students are changing and challenging student services. *Journal of College Student Development, 51*(2), 115–134.

Lloyd-Jones, E., & Smith, M. (1938). *A student personnel program for higher education.* New York, NY: McGraw-Hill.

Lloyd-Jones, E., & Smith, M. R. (1954). *Student personnel work as deeper teaching.* New York, NY: Harper & Brothers.

Manning, T. (2003). Leadership across cultures: Attachment style influences. *Journal of Leadership & Organizational Studies, 9*(3), 20–30.

Margolis, M. (1979). *Viable democracy.* New York, NY: St. Martin's Press.

Matsuda, M., Lawrence, C., Delgado, R., & Crenshaw, K. (1993). *Words that wound: Critical race theory, assaultive speech and the First Amendment.* San Francisco, CA: Westview Press.

McDade, T. (2005). For resident assistants: A race for inequality. *Chronicle of Higher Education, 50*(48), B5. Retrieved from http://chronicle.com/weekly/v50/i48/48b00501.htm

Merelman, R. (1984). *Making something of ourselves: On culture and politics in the United States.* Berkeley: University of California Press.

Mezirow, J., & Associates. (2000). *Learning as transformation: Critical perspectives on a theory in progress.* San Francisco, CA: Jossey Bass.

Mohanty, C. (1994). On race and voice: Challenges for liberal education in the 1990's. In H. Giroux & P. McLaren (Eds.), *Between borders* (pp. 145–166). New York, NY: Routledge.

Moore, M. (2001). *Stupid White men.* New York, NY: Regan Books.

Myers, L. (1993). *Understanding an Afrocentric world view: Introduction to an optimal psychology* (2nd ed.) Dubuque, IA: Kendall Hunt.

Noddings, N. (1988). An ethic of caring and its implications for instructional arrangements. *American Journal of Education, 96*(2), 215–230.

Noddings, N. (1990). Constructivism in mathematics education. *Journal for Research in Mathematics Education, 4*, 7–18.

Ogbu, J. (1990). Cultural models, identity and literacy. In R. Stigler, R. Schweder, & G. Herdt (Eds.), *Cultural psychology* (pp. 520–541). New York, NY: Columbia University Press.

Okun, B., Fried, J., & Okun, M. (1999). *Understanding diversity: A learning as practice primer.* Pacific Grove, CA: Brooks Cole.

O'Sullivan, E. (1999). *Transformative learning: Educational vision for the 21st century.* New York, NY: St. Martin's Press.

Parks, S. (2000). *Big questions, worthy dreams.* San Francisco, CA: Jossey-Bass.

Pascarella, E., & Terenzini, P. (2005). *How college affects students: A third decade of research.* San Francisco, CA: Jossey-Bass.

Patton, M. (1990). *Qualitative evaluation and research methods.* Newbury Park, CA: Sage.

Perry, W. (1968). *Forms of ethical and intellectual development in the college years: A scheme.* New York, NY: Holt, Rinehart & Winston.

Phelan, P., Davidson, A., & Hanh, C. (1993). Students' multiple worlds: Navigating the borders of family, peer and school cultures. In P. Phelan & A. Davidson (Eds.), *Renegotiating cultural diversity in American schools* (pp. 52–88). New York, NY: Teachers' College Press.

Pope, R., Reynolds, A., & Mueller, J. (2004). *Multicultural competence in student affairs.* San Francisco, CA: Jossey-Bass.

Public Broadcasting Service, & Merrow, J. (Producers). (2005). *Declining by degrees: Higher education at risk* [DVD]. United States: Public Broadcasting Service.

Readings, B. (1996). *The university in ruins.* Cambridge, MA: Harvard University Press.

Reason, R., & Broido, E. (2011). Philosophies and values. In J. Schuh, S. Jones, S. Harper, & Associates (Eds.), *Student services: A handbook for the profession* (5th ed., pp. 80–95). San Francisco, CA: Jossey-Bass.

Renn, K., & Arnold, K. (2003). Reconceptualizing research on college student peer culture. *Journal of Higher Education, 74*(3), 216–291.

Rentz, A. (Ed.). (1993). *Student affairs: A profession's heritage* (2nd ed.). Washington, DC: American College Personnel Association.

Sabine, G. (1961). *A history of political theory* (3rd ed.). New York, NY: Holt, Rinehart & Winston.

Saddlemire, G. L., & Rentz, A. L. (1986). *Student affairs: A profession's heritage.* American College Personnel Association, Washington, DC.

Scheffler, I. (1965). *Conditions of knowledge: An introduction to epistemology and education.* Chicago, IL: Scott, Foresman.

Schweder, R. (1990). Cultural psychology—what is it? In J. Stigler, R. Schweder, & G. Herdt (Eds.), *Cultural psychology: Essays on comparative human development* (pp. 1–46). New York, NY: Columbia University Press.

Seifert, T. (2007). Understanding Christian privilege: Managing the tensions of spiritual plurality. *About Campus, 12*(2), 10–17.

Shermer, M. (2002, September). The shamans of scientism. *Scientific American, 286*(6), 35.

Siegel, D. (2007). *The mindful brain.* New York, NY: Norton.

Specter of scientism. (2007). Retrieved from http://www.naturalism.org/scientism.htm

Steele, C. M., & Aronson, J. (1995). Stereotype threat and the intellectual test performance of African-Americans. *Journal of Personality and Social Psychology, 69*(5), 797–811.

Steffes, J., & Keeling, R. (2006). Creating strategies for collaboration. In R. P. Keeling (Ed.), *Learning reconsidered 2: A practical guide to implementing a campus-wide focus on the student experience* (pp. 69–74). Washington, DC: American College Personnel Association, Association of College and University Housing Officers-International, Association of College Unions-International, National Academic Advising Association, National Association for Campus Activities, National Association of Student Personnel Administrators, and National Intramural Recreational Sports Association.

Sue, D., Capodilupo, C., Torino, G., Bucceri, J., Holder, A., Nadal, K., & Esquilin, M. (2007). Racial microaggressions in everyday life: Implications for clinical practice. *American Psychologist, 6*(4), 271–286.

Takaki, R. (2008). *A different mirror* (Rev. ed.). Boston, MA: Little, Brown.

Taylor, M. (2010). *Crisis on campus: A bold plan for reforming our colleges and universities.* New York, NY: Knopf.

Terkel, S. (1992). *Race.* New York, NY: Doubleday.

Tocqueville, A., de. (1956). *Democracy in America* (R. Heffner, Trans.). New York, NY: Mentor Books. (Original work published 1835)

Tolstoy, L. (2011). *War and peace* (L. Maude & A. Maude, Trans.). Retrieved from http://tolstoy.thefreelibrary.com/War-andPeace (Original work published 1869)

Torres, V. (2003). Influences on identity development of Latino students in the first two years of college. *Journal of College Student Development, 44*(4), 532–547.

Trochim, W. M. (2000). *The research methods knowledge base.* Retrieved from http://www.socialresearchmethods.net/kb/

Tuchman, G. (2009). *Wannabe U: Inside the corporate university.* Chicago, IL: University of Chicago Press.

Wehlberg, C. (2008). *Promoting integrated and transformative assessment: A deeper focus on student learning.* San Francisco, CA: Jossey-Bass.

West, C. (1993a). *Race matters.* Boston, MA: Beacon Press.

West, C. (1993b). *Prophetic thought in post-modern times.* Monroe, ME: Common Courage Press.

Wheatley, M. (1999). *Leadership and the new science* (2nd ed.). San Francisco, CA: Berrett-Koehler.

Wilber, K. (2001). *Eye to eye: The quest for a new paradigm.* Boston, MA: Shambhala Press.

Yari, B. (Producer), & Haggis, P. (Director). (2005). *Crash* [Motion picture]. United States: Lionsgate Films.

Young, I. (1990). *Justice and the politics of difference.* Princeton, NJ: Princeton University Press.

Zakaria, F. (2008). *The post-American world.* New York: Norton.

Ziman, J. (1978). *Reliable knowledge.* London, UK: Cambridge University Press.

Zinn, H., & Arnove, A. (2004). *Voices of a people's history.* New York, NY: Seven Stories Press.

Zull, J. (2002). *The art of changing the brain.* Sterling, VA: Stylus.

Zull, J. (2006). Key aspects of how the brain learns. *New Directions for Adult and Continuing Education, 110,* 3–10.

CONTRIBUTORS

Craig John Alimo is a multicultural education specialist at the University of California, Berkeley in the Division of Equity of Inclusion, where he manages a multicultural education program. With the love, care, and compassion of his colleagues and friends, he is a social justice educator and has also taught undergraduate and graduate courses in social justice education content and process. He has also consulted with a variety of government, public, private, and nonprofit organizations. He can be reached at calimo@berkeley.edu.

Julie Beth Elkins is assistant dean of University College at Indiana University-Purdue University at Indianapolis. Elkins has provided national leadership in civic engagement through her research and former role as director of academic initiatives at Campus Compact. Elkins served as the spokesperson for corporate social responsibility at the University of Connecticut, where she provided national leadership for working with students on the Designated Supplier Program and was an elected member of the Workers' Rights Consortium. She can be reached at jelkins@iupui.edu.

Jane Fried is a professor in the Department of Counseling and Family Therapy at Central Connecticut State University where she directs the master's degree program in student development in higher education. She completed her doctoral course work at the University of Connecticut under the direction of Burns B. Crookston, who died unexpectedly in 1975. She earned her PhD in counseling psychology and human development from the Union of Experimenting Colleges and Universities. Fried is the editor of "Education for Student Development" (*New Directions in Student Services*, 15, 1981), *Different Voices: Gender and Perspective in Student Affairs Administration* (Washington, DC: Student Affairs Administrators in Higher Education, 1994), and "Ethics for Today's Campus: New Perspectives on Education, Student Development and Institutional Management" (*New Directions for Student Services*, 77, 1997). She is the author/editor of *Shifting Paradigms in Student*

Affairs: Culture, Context, Teaching and Learning (Alexandria, VA: American College Personnel Association; Lanham, MD: University Press of America, 1995), coauthor of *Understanding Diversity: A Learning as Practice Primer* (Pacific Grove, CA: Brooks/Cole, 1999), a contributing author of *Learning Reconsidered* (Washington, DC: American College Personnel Association and National Association of Student Affairs Professionals, 2004) and *Learning Reconsidered 2* (Washington, DC: American College Personnel Association and National Association of Student Affairs Professionals, 2006), and author of numerous articles and book chapters on ethics, diversity, spirituality, and learning. She has served on the executive council of American College Personnel Association as the chair of the Standing Committee on Women, the Committee on Ethics, and the Affirmative Action Committee. She can be contacted at friedj@ccsu.edu.

Scott Hazan is director of student activities/leadership development at Central Connecticut State University. He has also served as the student affairs representative on the First-Year Experience (FYE) Committee. He has helped develop a peer mentor program for the FYE program in which he coteaches peer mentoring. He can be contacted at hazanscz@ccsu.edu.

Elsa M. Núñez arrived as president of Eastern Connecticut State University with more than 20 years of previous experience as a senior administrator at such institutions as the University of Maine System and City University of New York. Núñez has a special interest in the recruitment, retention, and success of underrepresented student populations. Núñez previously worked for more than 20 years as an English professor at Ramapo State College in New Jersey.

Vernon Percy is an assistant professor at Central Connecticut State University. Percy has been an academic adviser to Division 1 teams and continues to work with sports programs that bring together Division 1 athletes with inner-city youths to provide mentoring and skill development. He can be contacted at percyver@ccsu.edu.

Christopher Pudlinski is a professor of communication at Central Connecticut State University. He has also served as faculty director of the First-Year Experience program at Central since 2008. His research interests include analyzing various methods of peer social support and exploring the organization and structure of consumer-run warm lines. He can be contacted at pudlinskic@ccsu.edu.

Sarah Stookey is an associate professor in the School of Business at Central Connecticut State University. She has worked extensively with agricultural cooperatives, nongovernmental organizations, and local governments in Nicaragua and elsewhere to develop democratic organizational structures and economic strategies. Her research interests are in the areas of management education, the social construction of money, and critical organization theory. She is founder of an innovative storefront, the student-directed community center of Central Connecticut State University in New Britain. She can be contacted at stookeysab@ccsu.edu.

James E. Zull is professor of biology and of biochemistry, and director of The University Center for Innovation in Teaching and Education (UCITE) at Case Western Reserve University. After 25 years of research on cell–cell communication, protein folding, cell membranes, and biosensors, he turned his interest toward understanding how brain research can inform teaching. Building on his background in cell–cell communication, his experience with human learning and teaching at UCITE, and drawing on the increasing knowledge about the human brain, led to writing his acclaimed first book, *The Art of Changing the Brain* (Sterling, VA: Stylus, 2002).

Also available from Stylus

Contested Issues in Student Affairs
Diverse Perspectives and Respectful Dialogue
Edited by Peter M. Magolda and Marcia B. Baxter Magolda

Contested Issues in Student Affairs augments traditional introductory handbooks that focus on functional areas (e.g., residence life, career services) and organizational issues. It fills a void by addressing the social, educational and moral concepts and concerns of student affairs work that transcend content areas and administrative units, such as the tensions between theory and practice, academic affairs and student affairs, risk taking and failure; and such as issues of race, ethnicity, sexual orientation, and spirituality. It places learning and social justice at the epicenter of student affairs practice.

The book addresses these issues by asking 24 critical and contentious questions that go to the heart of contemporary educational practice. Intended equally for future student affairs educators in graduate preparation programs, and as reading for professional development workshops, it is designed to stimulate reflection and prompt readers to clarify their own thinking and practice as they confront the complexities of higher education.

Student affairs faculty, administrators, and graduate students here situate these 24 questions historically in the professional literature, present background information and context, define key terms, summarize the diverse ideological and theoretical responses to the questions, make explicit their own perspectives and responses, discuss their political implications, and set them in the context of the changing nature of student affairs work.

Each chapter is followed by a response that offers additional perspectives and complications, reminding readers of the ambiguity and complexity of many situations.

Learning Partnerships
Theory and Models of Practice to Educate for Self-Authorship
Edited by Marcia B. Baxter Magolda and Patricia M. King

"Those interested in strengthening the ties between theory and practice and between faculty and student affairs can find inspiration here. Those committed to developing the co-curriculum to promote self-authorship will have a better sense of how to do that from this book. *Learning Partnerships* could serve as a text for courses on epistemological development or teaching and learning. It could provide a foundation for professional development for faculty or student affairs practitioners (and examples for doing so are included). . . . With its focus on practice and experiential education and its personal tone, readers are invited into the worlds of the authors to see the assumptions and principles of the [Learning Partnerships Model] in practice. With this volume, Baxter Magolda and King continue to make significant contributions to higher education and student affairs and encourage learning partnerships to promote students' development."—*Journal of College Student Development*

Demonstrating Student Success
A Practical Guide to Outcomes-Based Assessment of Learning and Development in Student Affairs
Marilee J. Bresciani, Megan Moore Gardner and Jessica Hickmott

"This volume is a wonderful addition to existing resources on assessment in student affairs. Its value is in its focus on a crucial form of assessment: demonstrating how student experiences contribute to the richness of undergraduate life. What's more, institutional illustrations and examples add robustness to this book through detailed treatment of central topics in outcomes assessment."—*John H. Schuh*, *Distinguished Professor, Iowa State University*

This practical guide to outcomes-based assessment in student affairs is designed to help readers meet the growing demand for accountability and for demonstrating student learning. The authors offer a framework for implementing the assessment of student learning and development and pragmatic advice on the strategies most appropriate for the readers' particular circumstances.

22883 Quicksilver Drive
Sterling, VA 20166-2102

Subscribe to our e-mail alerts: www.Styluspub.com